NIGHT LIFE

'The dream is an involuntary kind of poetry.'

CHARLES RYCROFT, *The Innocence of Dreams*

NIGHT LIFE

The Interpretation of Dreams

LIAM HUDSON

St. Martin's Press   New York

First published in the United States of America in
1985

ISBN 0-312-57287-5

Library of Congress Cataloging-in-Publication
Data

Hudson, Liam.
  Night life.

  Includes bibliographical references and index.
  1. Dreams.   I. Title.
BF1078.H83   1985   154.6'34   85-18315
ISBN 0-312-57287-5

Contents

Acknowledgements

More than most, this is a book dependent on the knowledge and open-handedness of others. I was introduced to Artemidorus by Keith Hopkins, and Ruth Padel has pointed me towards ancient sources. Adam Kuper sent me his paper on Freud's Irma dream, which has lent shape to my own argument at a point where this was previously lacking. The influence of Peter Hildebrand, with whom I teach a course on psychoanalytic explanations, has sharpened the discussion of Freud's dream theory; and for what understanding I possess of neural networks I am indebted to Igor Aleksander and Dr Francis Crick, both of whom have offered patient advice. John Odling Smee, John Richardson and Michael Wright, too, have read and commented upon chapters about which I felt nervous.

The Edinburgh sleep and dream-recall studies, although they appear towards the end of the book, are the kernel around which it grew. Carried out by Mark Austin and Michael Holmes, these demanded stamina as well as insight, and would in any case have been impossible had it not been for the shrewdness of Ian Oswald's advice, and his generosity in making available to us the facilities of his sleep laboratory.

Books about dreams not only tax one's knowledge, however; they have, built into them, a tendency towards chaotic dispersal. I am more than usually grateful, therefore, for the editorial wisdom and skills of my wife Bernadine Jacot, who has watched the text pass through a dozen guises, and of Robert Baldock, who has watched it pass through its last two.

CHAPTER ONE

Dreams and Meanings

The question of dreams and their meanings is an ancient one. In the past, dreams have been treated as a source of vitality and surprise, and as yielding insights quite unlike those gleaned from common sense. Whether through the intimacy of their links with the imagination and with fantasy, or through the fascinations of the apparently supernatural, dreams have been marked off from the everyday: familiar and yet at the same time strange – our nightly glimpse into a world of antic meanings from which we are otherwise excluded.

Our forebears seem to have been content for centuries to agree about the dream, or to agree at least to differ. As a result, a body of received wisdom about the dream evolved – one within which the views of experts and laymen coexisted in a state of drowsy acceptance and relative calm. But over the last hundred years or so – years of unprecedented technological advance, during which psychology has established itself as a discipline and more consciously rational attitudes to knowledge have become the dominant ones – this state of affairs has changed. Radically opposed views of the dream have been advanced, and some assaults on previously entrenched beliefs have been so violent that our very access to our dream experience has at times been threatened. Where, a century ago, men and women peered into their dreams as though they were visions of Aladdin's Cave, they are nowadays more likely to perceive them as gurglings in the mind's pipework; to view their dreams as they would their indigestion.

As a field of research, dreaming is consequently a turbulent one, and its excitements increase, year by year, as the conflicts between rival dream theorists become explicit. It is not just a field in which, to a flamboyant extent, experts disagree; it is one in which, amidst the clamour, the vigour of the dream itself is at risk. On the one hand, there are those, often psychoanalysts, who see dreams as encoded messages that we transmit to ourselves while asleep. The interpretation of such messages is a matter of cracking the relevant code. On the other, there are those who argue that dreams are nonsense – the scraps and tatters of meaning that the engine of human intelligence produces when it is thrown for the time being out of gear. This is the view often voiced by the scientifically trained: those who work in and around the sleep laboratory, and who make sense of the brain by treating it as an information-processing system, a species of soft computer.

This conflict of views cuts deep. It reflects the ritual antagonism that seems to have sprung up of its own accord in our culture between the artistically and scientifically inclined; the tender-minded and the hard-nosed. It also constitutes a special kind of challenge in that any reconciliation must take into account starkly opposed habits of mind and types of evidence: the material of the poet at one extreme, and that of the brain physiologist at the other. It is tempting to steer clear of all such conjunctions, but reconcile one must; and not just in the slovenly way that allows each protagonist his point of view, but by entering into the various kinds of evidence that the dream attracts, and arguing in detail for the elbow-room that a more satisfactory account requires.

The chapters that follow aim at just such a reconciliation. Their purpose is to outline a discipline or method of dream interpretation. To succeed, this must be compatible with the various sorts of knowledge about the dream that we now possess: scientific, psychoanalytic, literary. It must be orderly. And it must establish working principles within which the activity of dream interpretation can be contained.

Initially, the focus is on the tradition of dream interpretation established by the ancient Greeks, and assimilated in a modified form by the Victorians, among them the young Freud. The shortcomings of this 'Graeco-Freudian' tradition are examined with some care; in particular, the awkwardnesses that arise when experts advance interpretations of the same dream that sharply conflict. This view is then contrasted with its rude antithesis: the contention, advanced by behaviouristic psychologists, that the dream has no interpretable meaning whatever. This attack seeks to destroy the whole edifice of dream interpretation, and does so

2

on two grounds, one conceptual or philosophical, the other factual, a matter of new evidence about how the sleeping brain works.

The rest of the book is given over to the construction of a middle way. This accommodates what must be accommodated from thesis and antithesis, the psychoanalytic tradition and the scientists' counter-blast, and synthesises in that it takes arguments, familiar enough in themselves, and combines them in a way that is unfamiliar. It is a synthesis that is at root formal and procedural. It occupies a conceptual space different from that occupied by either brain research or the study of the unconscious as psychoanalysts have conceived it, yet it remains as compatible with the one as it does with the other.

This alternative view takes as its point of departure a remark of Charles Darwin, in which he compares the dream to poetry. He offers this more or less as an aside in the course of a discussion of the imagination.[1] Here, though, it is taken literally, and is used as the basis of a technique. If dreams are like poems, then an analysis of the dream can be conducted in terms of sentences that are dream-like in their effect. We can grasp the formal properties of the dream, which is both private and fugitive, by grasping those of the dream-like sentence – a text that is reassuringly public and that stays put. This method makes it possible to place the dream among a much wider array of thought processes that are dream-like, involuntary. It also leads to a discussion of ambiguity, the semantic property, above all others, that dream and poem share. Like many dreams, the poetic sentence consists of ideas and images that have several meanings rather than a single meaning, and yet are locked together into structures that are formally coherent.

This, then, is the first principle on which the discipline of dream interpretation is seen to stand: that the dream can be 'read' as though it were a poem – a skill that depends, crucially, on the notion of ambiguity and on a grasp of the distinction between ambiguity and muddle.

The second principle draws on an idea of great antiquity that has retained its vitality, namely that our first resort, in search of an interpretative thread with which to make sense of a dream, is to look for links with its waking context: those anxieties, doubts and fears that were governing the dreamer's mind in the hours or

3

days before he fell asleep. These daily residues are not the only ones on which a dream can draw – a chapter is devoted to some older ones – but they are those of most immediate use to the interpreter, and a reliance on them constitutes a hallmark of cautious interpretative practice.

The third principle is again somewhat Darwinian in tone. It rests on the claim that individuals differ. They differ in how they think while they are awake, in how they think while they are asleep, and in how they regulate the flow of ideas from one realm of thought to the other. In itself, this idea is not remarkable in the least. What is a little less ordinary is the belief that, far from being the nuisance most experimenters assume them to be, individual differences provide the variety on which our powers of adaptation depend.

The materials used in the discussion as a whole are varied, and intentionally so; dream reports, poems, paragraphs from novels, diagrams and laboratory experiments all find a place. This implies no retreat from the conventions of dispassion and rigour that underlie science, nor any wish to attack or deride its practices. Far from it. The aim here is in the widest sense 'scientific': it seeks to provide the phenomena of the dream with a mind-set that does them justice, and that could lead to a growth of understanding that is genuinely cumulative. As the chapter on individual differences shows, the laboratory is vital to this growth, in that it provides insights into the natural history of sleep and dreaming that no other source can match.

The discussion as a whole is loyal to scientific conventions in another respect too. It offers not a millimetre to those who make sense of dreams by invoking supernatural powers, who see them as portents, or who live in a world regulated by the extrasensory, occult or paranormal. Although it seeks to stretch the terms of reference within which many psychologists at present address the dream and its meaning, it is bounded by this self-imposed restriction.

While dealing unapologetically and in some detail with material that is bound to strike psychologists as unfamiliar, it is an argument addressed to an audience that is at heart broadly psychological: to those for whom the dream is inherently an object of fascination; to those eager to know how the imagination manages, against all odds, to subvert the dull tramp of habit; and

4

to the conceptually alert – those who realise that psychological explanation, the business of setting a thought to catch a thought, constitutes a mystery as strange in its way as dreaming itself.

It is also addressed to a smaller and more narrowly professional audience, though one that does seem to be growing: those of my fellow psychologists who realise that, fifty years of propaganda notwithstanding, the central issues of our trade are those of *meaning*,[2] and that, within the vast array of meanings that the human imagination generates, some of the most compellingly attractive are those 'texts' or 'signs' that convey intense or subtle feeling – some photographs, paintings and sculptures, certain film sequences, some passages of music, certain poems and passages of prose, and, of course, certain dreams. These are the texts that act, in William Gass's phrase, as 'containers of consciousness'.[3] They are cryptic and potent, ambiguous and enthralling. Never, or hardly ever, do they spell out their message in a literal-minded or pedestrian way.

The tasks of unpacking such containers, and of relating the needs and intentions of the person who fashions them to the needs and intentions of the person who receives them as audience, have scarcely begun. The peculiar fascination of the dream, in this context, is that artist and audience are one and the same.

Notes

(1) Darwin (1887), p. 74.
(2) For lack of better terms, the kind of study undertaken here is sometimes called 'hermeneutic', sometimes 'semiotic'. Hermeneutics is the discipline that has its origin in Biblical scholarship, and consists in the search for the best reading of obscure or corrupted texts. Semiotics, very much the property of the French sociologist Roland Barthes, is the study of signs. In fact, all such work is 'psychology', as properly understood: the '-logy' of the psyche, the study of the mind and its products. The question of whether such study constitutes a science is, I believe, an irrelevance. What matters is that it should be as orderly and as inventive as we can make it.
(3) Gass (1976), p. 86.

CHAPTER TWO

An Ancient Text

It is an oddity of the way in which we now write the history of ideas that we attribute to great men of the recent past a stature that obscures their predecessors. Accordingly, we take it for granted today that the dream's unconscious significance was discovered by Freud, as a feat of genius, performed without reference to his forebears. It comes as a shock, therefore, to find that in the second century AD a contemporary of Galen and Ptolemy was already approaching the activity of dream interpretation systematically.[1]

Artemidorus, about whom little is known, lived in Asia Minor and wrote in Greek. Not only are the five books of his *Oneirocritica* evidence of a sustained and powerful drive towards order, they also imply that his was one effort among many: that there existed a tradition of systematic dream interpretation in which he and his rivals had the status of experts.

And so it proves. In the centuries before Artemidorus, the Greeks had devoted time and ingenuity to the study of the dream, and had evolved attitudes towards it at least as various as the ones we hold today. The ancients treated the dream as an objective fact, an event in a world as real as that of waking experience. They also saw it as a message from the gods, expressed symbolically but subject to interpretation. In Homer, Dodds points out, these attitudes already coexisted, and did so without any apparent sense of strain.[2] In the fourth century BC, Hippocrates treats dreams as diagnostic aids to the physician, and interprets them more broadly in terms of a transformational code in which earth is the equivalent of flesh, a river the equivalent of blood, a tree the equivalent of the reproductive system, and so on. In these ancient times, it is worth noting, the Greeks never spoke of 'having' a dream, but of 'seeing' one; and dreams were said not only to 'visit' the dreamer but to 'stand over' him.

6

Aristotle, in contrast, is more sceptical. He denies that dreams are sent by the gods, claiming that if the gods wished to communicate with mankind they would be more careful in their choice of recipients. On the dream's power as a portent, he is cautious; more so than many since. He admits precognition in cases where patients allow into sleeping consciousness an awareness of symptoms ignored during the day, and also where dreams are self-fulfilling, in that they contain a suggested course of action that the dreamer subsequently follows. The rest he dismisses as coincidence, although he does make a concession of principle, suggesting that dreams originate in wave-borne stimuli, somewhat along the lines of ripples in water and currents in the air.[3]

Aristotle's good sense did not carry the day, though. Dream books flourished; and the Stoics revived the popular view of the dream as an objective visitation from the gods. Plutarch abstained from eating eggs because of certain dreams, and a surgeon as enlightened as Galen was prepared to perform an operation at the bidding of a dream.[4]

Artemidorus' *Oneirocritica*, in other words, has a solid historical context. As one turns the pages of its translation, one finds the apparently modern and the irredeemably ancient mixed together. Apparently modern is the tendency that Artemidorus shares with twentieth-century Marxists to see economic considerations as basic. Altogether more quaint is his assumption that the dream is a portent, a 'porthole' through which one can examine the future. In his work, the notion of the dream as god-sent is domesticated: its power to predict is retained and systematised, but this is now seen not so much as a matter of divine intervention as of the ordinary properties of the mind, a fact of life.

It may be that scholars will unearth mediaeval, renaissance or more recent texts that reveal an altogether richer pattern of evolution in our thought about the dream; but it does seem that the two millennia separating Artemidorus from the Victorians saw only slight changes in the ways that dreams were understood. The notion of the dream as a portent remained dominant: accepted as a fact by Artemidorus, it echoes through the literature of the intervening centuries. It is heard, for example, in Chaucer, and, as we shall see, it was to exert a

7

powerful influence over Jung and Freud.

When, in the fourteenth century, Chaucer's Troilus dreams that Cressida, 'my lady bryght', lies kissing a sleeping boar 'with tuskes grete', he assumes that she will betray him. Pandarus reassures Troilus that dreams are inscrutable: 'Lat be this thought; thow kanst no dremes rede.' But Cressida does go off in the end with the alien Greek, Diomede, and Troilus is killed by Achilles. Scepticism, we are being told, does not wash; dreams are portents after all.[5]

If Artemidorus' commitment to the idea of the portent was unremitting, so too was the urgency with which his mind moved towards an interpretative system. Like Freud's theory, and like many other constructions both inside science and out, the *Oneirocritica* is a feat of the imagination and will: a vision – or, to use the slang of modern science, a 'story' – that carries weight and conviction through the very urgency and persistence with which it is told. Rather than simply being a hypothesis about the natural order that is either true or false, it is an expression of the man, part of his identity. It commands our attention, even when muddled or mistaken, much as a work of art can.

There is a sense, in other words, in which the *Oneirocritica*, like any other theory about the dream, must belong to the class of phenomena it seeks to explain. It is a system that seems matter-of-fact, but is not. Rather, it is an idealised structure, a beautiful edifice, and belongs to a much wider category of visionary schemes, some of which are political, social, religious or scientific, some more intimately personal. Colloquially, all are 'dreams'. But a dream theory is a 'dream' of a special sort: a 'dream' about dreams. Such 'dreams' are often true in the sense that they are compelling or fertile, without necessarily being true at the level of fact – indeed, without at that level ever seriously being put to the test.

Artemidorus' self-imposed task strongly resembles that of the modern botanist. Faced with the bewildering variety of, say, flowering shrubs, the botanist classifies or taxonomises, dividing genus from genus, species from species. As with plants, so with dreams: such classificatory schemes always seem insecure. Plants – rhododendrons, for example – merge one with the other in nature, and with each new discovery the pressure for a change in the principles governing the classificatory scheme mounts.

8

The result is that, while the plants themselves are solid enough, the categories that are invoked to contain them, though reassuringly tidy, are oddly spectral.[6]

In translation, the five books of the *Oneirocritica* run to some 180 pages. Their argument assumes, with an almost hypnotic insistence, that dreams are propositions about the future. Some will be acted out literally, while others are riddles that have to be solved. This predictive capacity is seen as inherent in the mind's working. 'The mind', Artemidorus tells us, 'predicts everything that will happen in the future, whether the lapse of time in between is great or small, by means of images of its own, called elements, that are natural products.' This 'movement or condition of the mind' is called *oneiros*. It is a feature that 'is not a matter of controversy, for no one will ever deny that, directly after the vision itself . . . such things happen'. Indeed, some come true 'while we are still under the sway of the dream-vision'. A man who was at sea dreamt that he suffered shipwreck and later was actually wrecked: 'when sleep left him, the ship sank and was lost, and the man, along with a few others, narrowly escaped drowning.' Another dreamt that he was wounded by a man with whom he had agreed to go hunting: 'he set out with the man and was wounded by him in the shoulder where he had been wounded in the dream.' A third dreamt that he received some money from a friend. 'In the morning, he received ten minas as a deposit and he guarded it.'[7]

But dreams do not just come true for the dreamer; they offer glimpses into the future of others. 'For example, someone dreamt that he died. In real life, his father died.' 'Another man dreamt that he was beheaded. In real life, the father of this man, too, died.' Transpositions are also frequent: 'if a man dreams that his mother or wife is ill', this indicates that his business activities will be 'weak and disorganised'. Such a transposition makes sense, Artemidorus says, 'for all agree that it is consonant with reason that a craft corresponds to one's mother, since it nourishes, and to one's wife, since it is in the highest degree one's own'.

The interpreter's task, Artemidorus assumes, is that of separating the more likely interpretations from the less; the plausible from the far-fetched. Objective knowledge is not possible, and much depends on the interpreter's skill:

'Therefore I maintain that it is necessary for the interpreter of dreams to have prepared himself from his own resources and to use his native intelligence rather than simply to rely upon manuals, since a man who thinks that he will be perfect by theory without any natural talents will remain imperfect and incomplete, and all the more, the more set he is in this habit.'[8]

The interpretation of dreams is critically dependent too, Artemidorus believes, on a grasp of who does the dreaming. Thus,

'if a young woman dreams that she has milk in her breasts, it signifies that she will conceive, carry, and bring to birth a child. But for an old woman, if she is poor, it prophesies riches; if she is rich, it indicates expenses. For a maiden in the bloom of youth, it means marriage, since she could not have milk without sexual intercourse. But for a girl who is quite small and far from the time of marriage, it prophesies death. For all things, with few exceptions, that are out of season are bad.'[9]

In his choice of topics, Artemidorus ranges widely. Dreams of birds, child-birth, children, death, eating, feet, gods, gold, hands, heads, olives, penises, sickness, silver, strangers, vines, wheat, wives; all these are examined. Sexual intercourse is dwelt on too, but only as one area of concern among many. The discussion of sexual dreams in the *Oneirocritica* is of special interest to modern eyes, though, both for the elaboration of its detail, and in its dependence on notions of power and profit. For example, 'if a man dreams that he has sexual intercourse with his wife and that she yields willingly, submissively, and without reluctance to the union, it is good for all alike.' So much one might expect. But the reasoning behind this interpretation is unexpected: rather than psychological or moral, it is baldly political or economic. His wife, within Artemidorus' interpretative scheme, represents the man's craft or trade and all those things that lie entirely within his control. In his dream, he affirms his sovereignty over his own domain; an auspicious thing to do.

Intercourse with a prostitute presents greater interpretative difficulty. In general, it signifies 'a little disgrace' and 'a small expense'. On balance, though, it can still be auspicious, in that prostitutes give themselves without resistance. If a man dreams that he 'enters a house of prostitution' and can leave afterwards, the outlook is good; if he dreams that he enters and cannot then leave, it is bad – a man who dreamt that he went to a brothel and could not leave 'died a few days later'. This outcome is logical, in Artemidorus' view, both because a brothel, like a cemetery, is called 'a place men have in common', and because 'many human seeds perish there'; 'in a natural way, then, this place resembles death.'

If a man dreams that he has intercourse with a woman he does not know, this is auspicious, should the woman be willing, and should she also be 'pretty, and graceful and . . . attired in expensive, fine clothes'; it is inauspicious if she is ugly, deformed, shabbily dressed, old or unwilling. Sexual intercourse with a servant, male or female, is good, because slaves are possessions, and it is natural for a man to enjoy what belongs to him. Predictably, to be possessed by a household slave is inauspicious. The same holds for dreams in which a man is possessed by his brother, whether younger or older, or by a personal enemy. To be possessed by a richer, older man is good, 'for it is usual to receive things from such people'; to be possessed by someone who is younger or poorer is the reverse.

Thus far, the motifs of power and profit make Artemidorus' train of thought reasonably easy to follow. Surprises are in store when he turns to dreams of illegal intercourse. A dream of intercourse with another man's wife, even if freely given, is inauspicious because it brings into play the penalties of the law against adultery, which, needless to say, Artemidorus construes as an offence against property. If a man has intercourse with his son or daughter, the consequences are good or bad depending partly on the child's age. If the child is under five, the dream signifies the child's corruption and hence death. If more than five but less than ten, the child will be sick, because he or she is too young for intercourse and will experience pain, and the father will be disgraced in some way, because of his foolishness: 'no man with any self-control at all would possess either his own son or any other child of so tender an age.' If a son is grown up, intercourse is auspicious if the son is living abroad; inauspicious if he is living at home. To be forcibly possessed by one's son signifies injury by that son. In the case of grown daughters, though, the logic of interpretation takes a different path. 'It is good for a poor man to have sexual intercourse with a rich daughter,' because 'he will receive great assistance from his daughter and, in this way, take pleasure in her.' Rich fathers, on the other hand, give something to their daughters after such a dream; and if sick, may die, leaving their daughters their inheritance.

Artemidorus then addresses the intimacy of most pressing relevance to modern psychoanalytic thought: that of the dreamer with his own mother. 'The case of one's mother is both complex and manifold,' he warns, 'and admits of many different interpretations – a thing not all dream interpreters have realised. The fact is that the mere act of intercourse by itself is not enough to show what is portended. Rather, the manner of the embraces and the various positions of the bodies indicate different outcomes.' The outcome also depends on whether the mother is, in real life, living or dead at the time the dream occurs.

'Face-to-face intercourse' with a mother who is alive is auspicious, though it presages conflict with the father if he is alive too: auspicious because 'we ordinarily call a person's trade his "mother" ', and 'what else would having intercourse with her mean if not to be occupied with and earn one's living from one's art?'

If dreamer and mother are estranged, they will become friends again. But if the son is sick and his mother dead, the dream of intercourse signifies that he too will soon be dead. 'We speak of "Mother Earth", and what else would intercourse with a dead mother signify to a sick man if not that he will have intercourse with the earth?' That is to say, he will be buried. However, if the son would like to purchase land or to farm, the dream of intercourse with his dead mother augurs well; he will possess the earth he wants to possess. (Artemidorus acknowledges here a possible disagreement with other dream interpreters. For those who are already farmers, the dream could signify the casting of seeds on ground that is infertile: 'dead ground'. He falls back on the dreamer's reaction. If the dreaming farmer 'repents or is distressed by the intercourse', the signs are bad; otherwise, they are good.)

Questions of posture are telling too, though. 'It is not good to possess a mother who is looking away from one,' and it is also 'unlucky to have intercourse with one's mother while she is standing' – because men only use this position when they are too poor to have bed or mattress. 'Possessing one's mother from underneath while she is in the "rider" position' is usually benign: although sick men 'regularly die after this dream', those in good health 'spend the rest of their lives in great comfort and doing whatever they want'. This, he feels, is both 'natural and reasonable', because when the female is on top the male derives his pleasure without exertion. He will also 'escape the notice of others and remain undetected, since heavy breathing is for the most part eliminated'.

It is not auspicious to 'use many different positions on one's mother', because this insults her. Face-to-face intercourse is the natural method, and all others are aberrations, arising from 'wantonness, licentiousness, and intoxication'. The worst dream by far however is the one in which the dreamer 'practises *fellatio* with his mother'. This signifies the death of children, the loss of property and grave illness. Artemidorus claims to know of a man who, after this dream, 'lost his penis'.

The 'unnatural' is, likewise, a field in which Artemidorus advances his interpretations with steady purpose. A dream in which a man has 'sexual intercourse with himself' is disastrous for rich and poor alike. So too can be dreams of intercourse with gods or goddesses, and dreams in which one possesses or is possessed by a corpse. Sexual intercourse with animals is benign as long as the man mounts the animal, the benefits varying from animal to animal. If, however, the animal mounts the man, 'terrible acts of violence' are in store.

In his treatment of dreams about sex, Artemidorus combines what, from the vantage point of the twentieth century, must seem the strikingly contemporary with the remote. Modern is his even-handedness. He is free to catalogue states of mind that, within the very recent past, members of our own culture could view only through veils of embarrassment, even outrage. He is modern, too, in that he uses power so insistently, as modern Marxists and some feminists do, as his interpretative theme. He is old-fashioned, even Victorian, in that he pays little attention to the experience of women: they are dealt with only in passing, precisely because they lack power.

Even more compelling than these impressions, though, is a

further feature with which the *Oneirocritica* confronts us: the impression that in the intervening years our dreams have become tame. Looking down the list of dreams Artemidorus includes in his Fifth Book, offered as a manual of instruction to his son who he hoped would follow in his footsteps, one bizarre image succeeds another. His list begins with a man who dreamt that he 'was chained to the pedestal of Poseidon of the Isthmus' and who became a priest of Poseidon. Next comes a man who dreamt that 'he brought forward his own wife as a sacrificial victim, that he offered her up, cut her flesh in pieces, sold them, and made a very large profit.' He dreamt that he enjoyed what he had done and attempted to conceal the money he collected from the butcher's shop in order to avoid the envy of bystanders. (His wife was a prostitute and he lived off her immoral earnings, a source of profit that 'deserved to be hidden'.) Then comes a man who dreamt that the frame around a portrait of himself had fallen apart. He dreamt that he had said, 'My portrait is still intact but the frame is broken.' The frame, Artemidorus claims, represented the rest of his body; the portrait, his face: 'naturally, he went lame in both of his feet.'

Further down the list, one finds a man who 'dreamt that he flayed his own child and made a wineskin out of him'. On the following day, his child fell into a river and was drowned; 'for a wineskin is made from dead bodies and is capable of receiving liquids'. A woman dreamt 'that she had an eye in her right breast'; a man dreamt that 'he ate his own excrement with bread and enjoyed it' – and came into an inheritance by illegal means. There is a woman who dreamt that a handmaid in her service borrowed her portrait and her clothes. Soon afterwards, the handmaid destroyed this woman's marriage by slanderous means. There is a man who dreamt that Asclepius wounded him in the belly with a sword and that as a result he died. In real life, he developed an abscess in his belly and was cured after surgery.

Yet another man dreamt that 'he was feeding his penis with little bits of bread and cheese as if it were an animal.' He died a horrible death, because the food that he should have been giving to his mouth he was giving to his penis. And a woman dreamt that 'stalks of wheat sprouted from her breast' and 'bent back and went down into her vagina'. Through a mishap, she had sexual intercourse with her own child, and she committed suicide.

One man dreamt that 'he found many large bed bugs in his chiton'. Disgusted, he tried to shake them off but failed. Next day, he discovered that his wife was committing adultery, but owing to some unspecified impediment he could not divorce her. Another dreamt that 'he had a mouth and large, beautiful teeth in his rectum through which he spoke, ate, and did everything that is usually done by a mouth.' Through some 'unguarded remarks', this man was forced to flee his homeland and went into exile. A woman dreamt that she held in her hands her husband's severed penis. She took care that it should come to no harm. Later, she bore him a child, but still was divorced.

And so on. It may be that these dreams were culled by Artemidorus from an enormous number of reports, most of which were by comparison more humdrum. It is possible, too, that like a twentieth-century scientist writing up a research report he took it upon himself to simplify his material and heighten its effect, rather than to record it comprehensively, in its full prosaic detail.[10] Some he may have invented. The impression remains, nonetheless, that the citizens of the Holy Roman Empire not only enjoyed a daily life more brutal than any we countenance, but carried elements of this brutality over into the thinking they did while asleep. The assumption must be, in other words, that the dream is not a discrete fragment of experience, separate from the life we lead with our eyes open. It is complementary to that life; and it is a central feature of the psychologist's task to discover what the rules governing that complementary relationship might be.[11]

Notes

(1) Freud was both thorough and generous in acknowledging his debts, as the early chapters of *The Interpretation of Dreams* demonstrate. Regrettably, he also conspired with his followers to establish a myth of himself as hero, a creator in the romantic mould (Sulloway, 1979). Psychoanalysis apart, there does seem a broader tendency in subjects like psychology, sociology and linguistics either to treat the discipline as a science and to ignore its past as irrelevant, or to invest all wisdom in a few prophetic voices: Darwin and

Freud, Marx and Weber, Lévi-Strauss and Chomsky, Laing and Lacan.

(2) Dodds (1951), p. 104. Dodds's chapter on 'Dream-Pattern and Culture-Pattern' is admirably accessible. He also points out that a third attitude to the dream made 'a sensational first appearance' in the fifth century BC: the belief that the dream-vision is seen by the soul when out of the body, an event in a spirit world.

(3) Ibid., p. 120. Plato, in contrast, saw dreams as originating in the rational soul, but as being perceived by the irrational soul as images reflected on the smooth surface of the liver. Hence, their obscure symbolic character, and the need for interpretation.

(4) Ibid., p. 121.

(5) Robinson (n.d.), p. 556. The same moral is pointed in Sophocles' *Oedipus Rex*.

(6) As it happens, the traditional scheme for naming and classifying rhododendrons has been scrapped in its entirety by experts at the Botanical Gardens in Edinburgh, and replaced with a new one, or, more strictly, by two new ones, the first designed for botanists who study plants, and the second for the horticulturalists who breed and sell them. There have been interesting consequences. Experts have displayed anger, even outrage, towards one another; and certain plants, quite distinct in our gardens (for instance, *R. concatenans*) have been 'sunk' – that is to say, they have been deemed no longer to exist as a separate entity: Leslie (1980).

(7) White (1975). Unless specified, the quotations in the next few pages are from pp. 15–16 and 58–65.

(8) Ibid., p. 22.

(9) Ibid., p. 25.

(10) It is a stubborn fiction, among scientists themselves and among those who know nothing of science at first hand, that a scientific analysis consists of a wholly objective and complete summary of all data that the research in question generates. In the event, Herculean tasks of selection are performed as a matter of course, picking out 'signal' from 'noise', a 'story' from the 'rubbish' in which it is buried. This selective process is distinct in principle (if not always in practice) from the neglect or suppression of inconvenient

evidence, or from outright fraud.

(11) Dodds remarks that Artemidorus' scheme resembles that which has been in favour in Africa within the last fifty years or so, his argument being that patterns of dreaming change with patterns of culture: Dodds (1951), p. 134. Jaynes (1976) proposes something altogether more radical: that, as recently as the second millennium BC, men had no consciousness at all; they simply heard and obeyed voices. Corresponding to the change that has occurred since, he suggests, there may have been a shift in cerebral dominance from right to left hemisphere.

CHAPTER THREE

Freud's Contribution

On reflection, what does one make of the porthole theory of dreaming, presented by Artemidorus in its secular but none-theless thoroughgoing form? Can it really be that, as a matter of fact, dreams preview the shocks and excitements of the weeks that follow? The answer must be that they cannot. The porthole theory is an error that rests on the kind of blunder Oxford undergraduates were once encouraged to call 'category mistakes'. One cannot treat the future as though it were a film already made but not yet released, a novel written but still to be published. It cannot be 'read', even in the limited respects that the past can. The future is the realm of the actuary.

If resorts to the supernatural or occult are set aside, dreams can only be seen as portents if the dreamer is in a position, consciously or unconsciously, to influence what actually takes place. In *Man and his Symbols*, Jung cites the dream of a patient who dreamt that his doctor has died in a fire.[1] Unknown to him, the doctor was in fact suffering from a gangrenous fever which was soon to consume him. Jung accepts this as precognition, but clearly accepts the existence of the supernatural in doing so. Either the patient knew more than he acknowledged, or the dream was a coincidence, not a portent.

No such niceties of philosophical principle informed the dream books of the nineteenth century. When compared with the *Oneirocritica*, they seem in fact to have revealed a regression into naivety. Sulloway, in his review of the antecedents of Freud's dream theory, refers to these books as both 'countless' and 'cheap'.[2] Two methods of interpretation were in use. The first was the Biblical one. Here, dreams are considered as a whole in order to uncover their hidden, prophetic meaning. Thus Joseph interprets the Pharaoh's dream of seven fat cows that are followed and then eaten by seven thin cows as foretelling seven years of plenty in Egypt that are the prelude to seven years of famine. More common in Freud's day, Sulloway claims, were the analyses that broke each dream down, piecemeal, into a series of short messages that could then be deciphered according to a fixed cryptographic key – in which, for example, the receipt of a letter stands for trouble in store.

Both methods assume the kind of advance warning that is possible only if the future is already 'written'; a cast of mind that is playful yet polemic, half-serious yet at the same time fully serious, and that is as pervasive today as it was a hundred years ago. A recent edition of the *TV Times* magazine records the paranormal powers of its astrologer, Russell Grant:

> 'I dreamed of a platform sign saying Wigan, and a train with the first couple of carriages mutilated. A couple of days later, a friend said he was going to Blackpool. I knew his train went via Wigan and I told him either to cancel the trip, or to sit at the rear. True enough, that train was de-railed near Wigan and the first two carriages were wrecked.'

The scholarly concern of the *Oneirocritica* is stripped away, and something altogether less evolved is offered in its place: the 'seer' who depicts himself, at least for the purposes of entertainment, not as an expert but as someone with mysterious powers, 'better' eyes.[3]

Sulloway acknowledges that, although they were readily available to him, there is no evidence that Freud actually consulted the popular dream books of his day. On the other hand, evidence exists that as a young doctor Freud kept notebooks of his dreams, and that, in these, he analysed dreams as possible portents. In a letter to his fiancée Martha Bernays, written in 1883 when he was twenty-seven, Freud reports a blissful dream of a landscape 'which according to the private notebook on dreams which I have composed from my experience indicates travelling'. It was not until 1925, twenty-five years after its publication, that he deleted from *The Interpretation of Dreams* a footnote ascribing 'prophetic' significance to one of the symptoms in his dream of Irma's injection (see Chapter 8).

Freud, then, was a creature of his time. Around him, the rudiments of the psychoanalytic theory of dreams, now indissolubly linked to his name, were taking shape. The analysis of the dream, Freud was to proclaim, is 'the royal road to a knowledge of the unconscious activities of the mind'; the dream itself he saw as the disguised fulfilment of a suppressed or repressed wish – usually, if not invariably, sexual in origin. Others, as he readily acknowledges in *The Interpretation of Dreams*, had had such ideas before him. The psychiatrist Wilhelm Greisinger, forty years earlier, had maintained that dreams share with psychoses the common feature of being the imagined fulfilment of wishes. Albert Moll was one of several to link dreams explicitly to sexuality, reporting, for instance, that when perverts are cured of their sexual aberrations, they often continue to dream of sexual experiences that are perverse. Fliess, too, was preoccupied with the question of sexuality.

The notion of the dream as a symbol – central to Freud's system – was explored in some detail by Karl Albert Scherner, whose *The Life of the Dream* was published in 1861. Freud acknowledges him as the 'true discoverer of symbolism in dreams'. Like Moll and others, Scherner was particularly interested in dream symbols of sexual significance. Alfred Maury, a contemporary of Scherner, introduced an experimental method of investigating dreams, instructing his assistant to stimulate him with smells and sounds while he was asleep. On being awakened, Maury recorded the dreams that had ensued: the smell of scent elicited, for instance, a dream in which he was in a perfume shop in Cairo. Maury was also at pains to relate his dream images to experiences in the past, ones long forgotten.

Hervey de Saint-Denys, whose *Dreams and the Means of Directing Them* was first published in 1867, evolved an even more exacting method of self-analysis.[4] He trained himself to wake after each dream in the course of a night, and disciplined himself, too, to alter the course that his dreams took while they were still unfolding. In his use of the concepts of condensation and displacement he anticipated Freud in a more technical way.

Others had developed the view that the dream not only embodies hidden meanings but fulfils psychological functions. The Englishman, James Sully, was one who saw the dream as a state in which we regress, conserving earlier systems of personality, earlier habits of response: 'When asleep we go back to the old ways of looking at things and of feeling about them, to impulses and activities which long ago dominated us.'

20

In all these antecedents of Freud's mature theory, we see the gathering together of threads. The dream was a topic in the air, and had been so since the 1860s. The prior conditions existed for a statement about dreams that would be sustained, systematic and memorable. Freud's feat was thus as much one of co-ordination and integration as it was one of discovery.

'Insight such as this falls to one's lot but once in a lifetime,' Freud was to write thirty years later in the preface to the third English edition of *The Interpretation of Dreams*. And he especially prized the insights it contained, he seems to suggest, because he stumbled across them by luck. Ernest Jones, his biographer, refers to the episode in question as a 'perfect example of serendipity'. Free-associating, Freud's patients began of their own accord to tell him of their dreams. It occurred to him that their dreams were like symptoms; and that, like symptoms, they were laden with scrambled meanings that it was his task to unscramble. It was from this initial conjunction of dreams with neurotic symptoms – an unfortunate one, Charles Rycroft has suggested – that the format of orthodox Freudian therapy was to evolve.[5]

The indications are, however, that the development of Freud's thinking about dreams actually followed a more complex and interesting path. A good recaller of his dreams, Freud kept dream notebooks, as his letter to Martha Bernays records. In the decade which separates this letter from his *Project for a Scientific Psychology*, written in 1895, Freud's thinking about dreams was to undergo two sorts of shift. It was natural, working as a neurologist, concerning himself with the central nervous system, that his mind should turn to mechanisms, and to the idea of the brain as a system within which complex functional relationships could be mapped. It was also natural, granted the climate of his time, that he should begin to see dreams as symbols laden with messages not about the future but about the past – ones in which old dramas, past crises, are re-enacted in disguised form. There is a sense, in other words, in which Freud's was to remain a porthole theory. What changed was the view the porthole afforded: where once it allowed us to peer into the future, it now allowed us to peer into the past.

Like most theories, Freud's altered somewhat over time. Its essentials, though, are these. At its root is the distinction he drew

21

between two principles of mental functioning, a distinction that, as Rycroft says, was in his own view the most important, the most seminal and the most revolutionary idea he ever had. One principle – the 'primary' – is characteristic of our sleeping thought and of the processes whereby our neurotic symptoms take shape; the other – the 'secondary' – characterises our waking thought. These two principles are different and opposed.

The primary processes are two: condensation, in which mental images fuse with one another, and displacement, in which one image replaces another and serves to symbolise it as it does so. These primary processes equate opposites, dissolve categories of time and space, and are in essence wish-fulfilling. The secondary processes, in contrast, obey the laws of grammar and logic, they respect the categories of time and space, they preserve opposites, and in essence they are adapted to the demands made upon the individual by the external world. It was also Freud's view, as his choice of terms suggests, that the primary processes are established before the secondary ones. They are the ones we have as infants, the secondary processes taking shape gradually as we are transformed from baby to adult.

It follows from this view that the dream is in some important sense abnormal. It is a specific event, too, rather than simply being a glimpse of mental activity that continues at night; and it has a specific function – that of expressing in hallucinatory but disguised form wishes that cannot find a place in the fabric of secondary thought.

Each day, our waking thought leaves behind it loose ends or residues: 'I never dream', Freud wrote, 'about matters that have occupied me during the day, only of such themes as were touched on once in the course of the day and then broken off.'[6] These residues become linked to the infantile wishes and memories with which our minds are stocked. Residues, old memories and repressed wishes then coalesce into a dream in its first, latent, form. The latent dream, however, is too outrageous to be experienced; and at a level before consciousness – the 'preconscious' – it is blocked by a censor. The 'dream-work' then begins.

The dream-work, the core of Freud's theory, is the unconscious process of thought whereby the latent dream is translated into a form that the censor will accept. Freud seems to have envisaged the dream-work as extending over many hours, into our waking as well as our sleeping lives; 'the dream-work', as Sulloway puts it, 'is set in motion during the previous day by experiences that elicit unconscious wishes. When sleep finally sets in, the pace of the dream-work is merely accelerated.' All this occurs unconsciously. The action of the dream-work, indeed its very existence, can only be inferred.

The dream-work was one of the components of his theory about which Freud changed his mind. Initially, he seems to have seen it as consisting of the primary mechanisms, condensation and displacement, and as explaining the symbolic nature of dreams. He later added a third and subsidiary mechanism, 'representation', in which abstract ideas are translated into specific, and often visual, form. Later still, influenced he claimed by Stekel, a fourth mechanism was added: 'symbolisation'.[7] Although symbolisation is an idea closely akin to representation, Freud appears to have granted it a separate status within his system. For where representation is one of the devices whereby raw and shocking dreams are rendered acceptable to the censor, symbolisation short-circuits the censor altogether; if expressed in symbolic form, repressed ideas need no disguise. It is not clear, as a consequence, whether symbolisation really qualifies as part of the dream-work, or whether it is, in effect, an alternative to it – whether two routes lead from the forbidden wish to the experience of dreaming, or only one.

Such uncertainties aside, the dream's path to consciousness is still incomplete, for once the dream-work is over and the dream's disguise is adequate, a further editorial pruning ensues. Freud refers to this as 'secondary revision'. Only when this is finished can the dream be uttered into consciousness, where it is experienced 'like a firework', which has taken hours to prepare, but 'goes off in a moment'.

Faced with such a theory, a cat's cradle of interlocking ideas, one is tempted to tamper. The three layers of psychic activity (unconscious, preconscious and conscious); the two – or is it three? – editorial processes in play (dream-work, symbolisation and secondary revision); the tension, more generally, between generative mechanisms and censoring ones: all this invites new and more elaborate flow charts and diagrams. It is also tempting to recast the theory in more modern-sounding terms; those of

Freud's Dream Theory

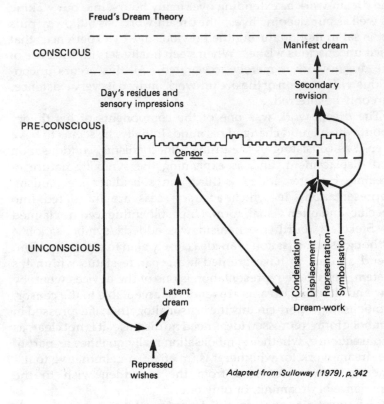

Adapted from Sulloway (1979), p. 342

computer programming, say, or of linguistics. But such academic tinkerings have their cost. The strangeness of the dream, its capacity to shock or haunt, can easily be lost from sight, its feral energy and the rudeness of its assault on common sense can be turned aside.[8]

In practice, however, the reputation of a theory like Freud's does not depend on niceties of detail. If he had been tidier, he would no doubt have been less influential. The attractions of his theory must lie not in the inevitability of its internal logic, but in its status as revelation: its promise of a new order which is more exciting than order itself.

Any such promise is dependent on its examples. For not only does the theory as it has so far been described fail to specify which interpretations are going to be the correct ones, it does not even specify the ground-rules in terms of which such decisions are going to be reached. How does one identify the correct interpretation of a dream which, as Freud acknowledges, may have several meanings and fulfil several quite different wishes? How does one separate the true reading or readings from the alternatives 'always lurking at the edge of every psychoanalytic interpretation'?[9] As it stands, the theory is a backdrop, and it is in front of this that the activity of interpretation is performed.

But consider the dream that Freud selected as his prime example; that of Irma's injection. Freud uses this as his specimen dream in *The Interpretation of Dreams*, and told his friend Fliess of his fantasy that a plaque would be erected on the summer house where he dreamt it:

> In This House, on July 24th, 1895
> the Secret of Dreams was Revealed
> to Dr. Sigm. Freud

It is beyond all serious question that Freud viewed his dream of Irma's injection as profoundly illuminative. All the more surprising, then, is the dream itself. It is discussed at some length in Chapter 8: it is sufficient to say here that, in Freud's hands, it contradicts the theory it is supposed to exemplify. It does not express a repressed wish – or at least not a repressed wish that is in any detectable sense sexual. On the contrary, it expresses Freud's anxieties about a patient of his, Irma, whose treatment had gone gravely awry, and about which Freud may well have begun to fear a professional scandal.[10]

The dream of Irma's injection seems to fall, in other words, into that class of sudden insights that are wonderful in their clarity, that the individual remains loyal to over a lifetime, that lead to discoveries that may well be solid enough, but that are themselves mistaken. Centuries before, the astronomer Kepler was seized in the same way by his vision of geometrical solids as the universe's invisible skeleton. Like Freud, he remained faithful to it throughout his career, and used it as his inspiration in establishing his three laws, and in his demolition of the ancient model of the universe based on wheels. Yet his vision was wrong. More than that, by the time he had completed his mature work, he had undermined practically every point that his original vision had expressed. Its value to him was undimmed, though, and his faith in it may well explain the extraordinary tenacity with which he pursued his calculations about the orbit of Mars, muddle succeeding muddle, error cancelling out error, until the correct solution – an ellipse – was achieved.[11]

Puzzling though this may initially seem, Freud's overriding commitment as a psychologist was to theories and to theory-building. He was also a stern rationalist, and his dedication to the rule of law was comprehensive. Far from relishing the unruliness of the sadistic and sexual fantasies he described, he was committed to their regulation. He believed in the therapeutic power of rationality, and he believed too in a social order in which the rational was sovereign: 'the ideal condition of things', he once wrote, 'would of course be a community of men who had subordinated their instinctual life to the dictatorship of reason.'

Dream analysis, and psychoanalysis more generally, was thus in Freud's hands an exercise in the Apollonian virtues: 'What interests me is the separation and breaking up into its component parts' of what would otherwise 'flow together into a primeval pulp'. 'We liberate sexuality through our treatment,' he wrote, 'not in order that man may from now on be dominated by sexuality, but in order to make a suppression possible – a rejection of the instincts under the guidance of a higher agency.' Accordingly, he saw psychoanalysis as a 'struggle between the doctor and the patient, between intellect and instinctual life, between understanding and seeking to act'; a struggle, more-over, in which 'the moral self was the conscious, the evil self was the unconscious'. As he was to put it when an old man: 'Where id was, there shall ego be'.[12]

These properties of Freud's mind are all the clearer when one compares him with Jung. In retrospect it seems natural that they should initially have been drawn to one another, but natural too that they should eventually quarrel. In his attitude to the unconscious Jung was altogether less embattled. He was happy to admit that 'the psychological treatment of the sick is a *relationship* in which the doctor is involved quite as much as the patient':

'If I wish to treat another individual psychologically at all, I must for better or worse give up all pretensions to superior knowledge, all authority and desire to influence. I must perforce adopt a dialectical procedure consisting in a comparison of our mutual findings.'

Jung extends his respect to the mad as well as to the neurotic: 'we cannot simply extract [a patient's] morbidity like a foreign body, lest something essential be removed along with it, something meant for life. Our task is not to weed it out, but to cultivate and transform this growing thing until it can play its part in the totality of the psyche.' It is one of many ironies surrounding modern psychoanalysis that Freud's name should be identified with liberalising beliefs that were the opposite of those he in fact held, while Jung, who in many respects anticipates contemporary attitudes, is assumed to have been an irrelevance.

Through the very steeliness of his dedication to the values of science, we might expect Freud to have been even-handed: to be as explicit about his own inner workings as he was about other people's. Again, though, we would be naive. Freud, in fact, was unusually skilled in covering his tracks. Many of the dreams in *The Interpretation of Dreams* are his own, but he edits his account of them so as to remove any violation of his privacy. Systematically, he also expunged all trace of the false-starts and hesitations through which his own ideas grew. Twice in the course of his adult life, once in his late twenties and again when he was forty, Freud destroyed all his manuscripts, private diaries, notes and correspondence. He did this, as a letter to Martha makes clear, with the judgement of posterity in view:

'I couldn't have matured or died without worrying about who would get hold of those old papers. . . . As for the biographers, let them worry, we have no desire to make it too easy for them. Each one of them will be right in his opinion of "The Development of the Hero", and I am already looking forward to seeing them go astray.'[13]

This, then, is the nub of the apparent contradiction that Freud's dream theory embodies. He spoke of dreadful things, but did so in the spirit of a coloniser. As he grew older, this commitment to the regulation of a dangerous world became increasingly obvious, and, the while, the apparent objectivity of the research worker dropped away. Jones quotes Freud's appraisal of himself: 'I am not really a man of science, not an observer, not an experimenter, and not a thinker. I am nothing but by temperament a *conquistador* – an adventurer, if you want to translate the word – with the curiosity, the boldness, and the tenacity that belong to that type of being.'[14] As so often in Freud, the metaphorical system at work is military: the control in question is not administrative so much as that of armed subjugation. He theorised about things that ordinary mortals could not bring themselves to mention, but did so in a heroic – some might say obsessive – attempt to render the dangerous safe.

Given Freud's intellectual vitality, his urge to regulate and his dedication to theory-building, a problem is then posed. The interpretation of the dream, its translation from the primary to the secondary mode, can become so comprehensive as to constitute a defence: a device for blocking access to the mind's more antic potentialities that is all the more subtly invasive for seeming so enlightened. As Malcolm Bowie says, in expounding Lacan's views, 'The discovery of the unconscious is itself subject to repression.' The unconscious is 'immobilized and domesticated by its professional observers. This extraordinary agent of dispersal and surprise becomes an ordinary counter within an ordinary conceptual game.' Lacan, Bowie claims, presents Freud as a 'new Actaeon turned upon and savaged by his own thoughts for having unveiled the goddess of the unconscious'. Lacan's self-appointed task, closely adjacent to that of the surrealists in painting and poetry, is, in contrast, to 'keep on thinking the intolerable Freudian thought, even at the price of dismemberment, and to allow repressed doctrine to make its disruptive return to psychoanalysis as it is performed and thought'.[15]

The task of maintaining a satisfactory bond between the dream and its interpretation, the antic and the patiently sober-sided, is one that is lost from sight, in Lacan's work, in a welter of Gallic convolution. It remains at the heart of the psychologist's activity, even so. Despite their dissimilarities, dream thought and deliberative intelligence must somehow remain intimately in touch, informing and invigorating one another, rather than being lodged in separate compartments, in a state of mutual insulation. A more humdrum, Anglo-Saxon suggestion about the nature of this relationship is set out at the end of the next chapter. Meanwhile there are severe embarrassments to be faced and overcome.

Notes

(1) Jung (1964), p. 78. More subtly marginal is Graham Greene's suggestion that as dreams and novels come from the same unconscious source, both can prefigure real events – their author's death, for instance: Greene (1981), p. 198. His friend Evelyn Waugh's death, he observes, was a re-run of scenes so often enacted in Waugh's books: 'it was a curious and in a way macabre death, which almost symbolised his work and his problems. It was Easter Sunday; he had been to Communion, he was lunching with his family, a priest was in the house – this can all represent the Catholicism to which he was so deeply attached – and he died in the lavatory: which represents his satire and the comic savagery with which he sometimes describes the deaths of his characters, and brings to mind Apthorpe's thunderbox in *Men at Arms*.' The suggestion is not that Waugh engineered his own death, only that the habits of thought that an author like Waugh found it natural to employ in writing could have shaped his actions when the time came for him to die.

(2) Sulloway (1979), on whom I have drawn heavily in writing this chapter.

(3) *TV Times*, for the third week in November, 1982.

(4) Saint-Denys (1981). His was the first account of 'lucid' dreams, those in which the dreamer knows that he is dreaming.

(5) Rycroft (1979), pp. 8–31. Rycroft's book gives an authoritative account, clear and civilised, of modern psychoanalytic thought about the dream. My own view, though not psychoanalytic in origin, owes much to it.

(6) Quoted by Jones from a letter Freud wrote as early as 1882: Sulloway (1979), p. 321.

(7) Ibid., p. 337; Rycroft (1979), p. 159. As Rycroft points out, the first edition of *The Interpretation of Dreams* contains only one sexually symbolic dream. It was not until the fourth

edition, in 1914, that a section on symbolism appears for the first time. Viewed coldly, this aspect of Freud's theory is a mess. Confusion was deepened, in the fifty years following the publication of his theory, by his followers' addiction to spot-the-symbol: the interpretative game in which all pointed objects are penises, all domed ones breasts, all declivities vaginas. It was as if Freudian analysts had access to a lexicon of true meanings which they dispensed as facts, as unproblematic as readings from the table of chemical elements.

(8) The dream-work can be spoken of in terms of metaphor and metonymy, for instance; and the unconscious can be treated more broadly as though it were constructed like a language, a view associated particularly with Jacques Lacan: Bowie (1979).

(9) Rieff (1959), quoted by Sulloway (1979).

(10) Kuper and Stone (1982).

(11) Koestler (1959); also Hudson (1966). Equally remarkable was the critic John Ruskin's obsession with the works of the painter Turner, another strangely misplaced but supremely productive passion: Hudson (1982).

(12) Roazen (1975), pp. 161–2, 272–5.

(13) Sulloway (1979), p. 7.

(14) Jones (1961), p. 227.

(15) Bowie (1979), p. 119. For readers baffled by Lacan's published works, Bowie is an informed and eloquent guide.

CHAPTER FOUR

Conflicting Claims

The elaboration of Freud's dream theory may seem remote from the interpretative concerns of the *Oneirocritica*. In fact, Freud shares with Artemidorus not only the belief that some unequivocal reading of the dream is possible, but also his faith in the existence of procedures for cracking the code.

In Freud's case, this procedure was of necessity out of the ordinary. He was committed by his theory to the distinction between the manifest and latent dream, the manifest dream being in disguise precisely because its real meaning was too shocking to be understood. As his method of penetrating this disguise, he chose free association. These associations, offered unreflectively by the dreamer to his analyst – or, in Freud's case, by the analyst to himself – constitute a series of hints. Characteristically, one association leads to another, to form an associative chain. It was from these that a grasp of the dream's true meaning was constructed. Though opening the floodgates to deception and self-deception, the method was justified at the time in terms of its results: it was seen as leading into the hidden landscape of the unconscious and to interpretations that were, in effect, descriptions of what that landscape contains.

Of course, there is no guarantee that one such landscape exists. Freud's method, as a result, was soon challenged. Quite quickly, too, analysts discovered that their interpretations diverged sharply; and it was in the apparent impossibility of resolving such disagreements rather than in any formal imperfections of theory that the central flaw of the 'Graeco-Freudian' tradition proved to lie.

The nature of this flaw is plain if one looks at the disagreements that arose between Freud and his younger colleague and later rival Jung. First, the question of method. Jung accepts that the dream often has a structure, and that this expresses an underlying idea or intention. But instead of following the paths of free association, which are likely to lead from the dream towards one of the dreamer's stable neurotic preoccupations, he urges the interpreter to concentrate upon the form and content of the dream itself. It is not the association of ideas as such that Jung objects to, but association that is free.

This insight Jung describes as a turning-point in the development of his own psychology:

'From this line of reasoning, I concluded that only the material that is clearly and visibly part of a dream should be used in interpreting it. The dream has its own limitation. Its specific form itself tells us what belongs to it and what leads away from it. While free association lures one away from that material in a kind of zigzag line, the method I evolved is more like a circumambulation whose centre is the dream picture. I work all around the dream picture and disregard every attempt that the dreamer makes to break away from it. Time and time again, in my professional work, I have had to repeat the words: "Let's get back to your dream. What does the *dream* say?".'[1]

Where Freud sees the dream as a door, and is eager to walk through it, Jung sees it as a text, and insists that we return to it, time and again, in the hope of teasing loose its secrets.

Disastrously, Jung then cites in his own support an example of dream interpretation that violates his own excellent precepts. A man dreams that his wife, a respectable woman, is drunken, dishevelled, vulgar. Jung, no less ardent a theoriser than Freud, concludes that because its representation of the wife is so obviously false, the dream must signify the existence, within the dreamer, of a female component that is slatternly – a hidden part of the personalities of all men that Jung called the 'anima', and that embodies an 'inferior kind of relatedness' to the world at large and especially to women. There is no reason why dreams should not be used to make theoretical discoveries. But, patently, Jung is here ignoring what the dream says: that the wife, despite her respectability, is perceived by her husband as drunken, dishevelled and vulgar – a view of her that he could well have formed, in spite of his better judgement, when in bed with her, or when watching her eating and drinking, or when thinking about her bodily functions. In his dream he could have been expressing a sense of distaste which an idealised perception of his wife was serving to disguise: precisely the kind of insight, one would have thought, on which the effective use of dream interpretation in therapy so often depends.

Despite such lapses, Jung's criticism of the free-association method is persuasive. Followed conscientiously, his own method is as cautious as Freud's was risky, and is, as it happens, neatly compatible with the analysis of more tangible texts and signs that I attempt later.

An advantage of Jung's approach is that it dispenses with Freud's distinction between manifest and latent dream. 'I was never able to agree with Freud', Jung says,

> 'that the dream is a façade behind which its meaning lies hidden – a meaning already known but maliciously, so to speak, withheld from consciousness. To me dreams are a part of nature, which harbours no intention to deceive, but expresses something as best it can, just as a plant grows or an animal seeks its food as best it can. . . . When Freud asserts that the dream means something other than what it says, this interpretation is a polemic against the dream's natural and spontaneous presentation of itself, and is therefore invalid.'[2]

This disagreement between the two men was thus not purely or even primarily a matter of method. It reflected their differing views of the dream itself; and from those differing views different sorts of interpretation flowed.

When he was four, Jung had a dream, a frightening one, that was to preoccupy him for the rest of his life. Here, he describes it from the vantage point of old age.

> 'The vicarage stood quite alone near Laufen castle, and there was a big meadow stretching back from the sexton's farm. In the dream I was in this meadow. Suddenly I discovered a dark, rectangular, stone-lined hole in the ground. I had never seen it before. I ran forward curiously and peered down into it. Then I saw a stone stairway leading down. Hesitantly and fearfully, I descended. At the bottom was a doorway with a round arch, closed off by a green curtain. It was a big, heavy curtain of worked stuff like brocade, and it looked very sumptuous.

Curious to see what might be hidden behind, I pushed it aside. I saw before me in the dim light a rectangular chamber about thirty feet long. The ceiling was arched and of hewn stone. The floor was laid with flagstones, and in the centre a red carpet ran from the entrance to a low platform. On this platform stood a wonderfully rich golden throne. I am not certain, but perhaps a red cushion lay on the seat. It was a magnificent throne, a real king's throne in a fairy tale. Something was standing on it which I thought at first was a tree trunk twelve to fifteen feet high and about one and a half to two feet thick. It was a huge thing, reaching almost to the ceiling. But it was of a curious composition: it was made of skin and naked flesh, and on top there was something like a rounded head with no face and no hair. On the very top of the head was a single eye, gazing motionlessly upwards. It was fairly light in the room, although there were no windows and no apparent source of light. Above the head, however, was an aura of brightness. The thing did not move, yet I had the feeling that it might at any moment crawl off the throne like a worm and creep towards me. I was paralysed with terror. At that moment I heard from outside and above me my mother's voice. She called out, "Yes, just look at him. That is the man-eater!" That intensified my terror still more, and I awoke sweating and scared to death. For many nights afterwards I was afraid to go to sleep, because I feared I might have another dream like that.'[3]

What did it mean? Over the years, Jung was to reach a considered view of it. 'Through this childhood dream', he says,

'I was initiated into the secrets of the earth. What happened then was a kind of burial in the earth, and many years were to pass before I came out again. To-day I know that it happened in order to bring the greatest possible amount of light into the darkness. . . . My intellectual life had its unconscious beginnings at that time.'

Jung concedes that what he saw in that underground chamber was a 'ritual phallus', but his comments about it are characteristically cerebral, dwelling on the etymology of the word 'phallus' in Greek. The effect is one of unsatisfactory vagueness. Jung seems to be obfuscating, somewhat as Freud had done over the dream of Irma's injection. Certainly, one of his biographers, Vincent Brome, will have none of it. For Brome it is self-evident that the hole in the meadow is a vagina, the underground chamber with the tree growing inside it is symbolic of sexual intercourse between mother and father Jung. The terror of the dream, the tree-turned-to-worm coming towards him, stands for his horror of the primal scene, fuelled in little Carl's mind by the domestic discord that his mother and father in fact endured. Where, in later life, Jung moved in his interpretative efforts towards myth and etymology, Brome relies on what he treats as the basic tenets of the psychoanalytically alert: the notions of infantile sexuality, the Oedipus Complex, sexual symbolism, the primal scene.[4]

It *is* quite possible that Jung was obfuscating. His interpretative elaborations could well have been defensive in inspiration; and, over the course of the years, his recollection of his dream and his theories of the mind could both have altered to achieve a better 'fit', one with the other. Brome's reading, the more orthodoxly Freudian one, is less speculative in tone. But who is to say that one is more secure than the other?

The hazards surrounding the search for a single correct reading become all the more obvious when one examines a dream that was a source of explicit contention between Jung and Freud himself. In 1909, sailing with Freud and Ferenczi to America on board the *George Washington*, Jung dreamt again of underground chambers. The dream was important to him because it led, for the first time, towards his notion of the collective unconscious.

'This was the dream. I was in a house I did not know, which had two storeys. It was "my house". I found myself in the upper storey, where there was a kind of salon furnished with fine old pieces in rococo style. On the walls hung a number of precious old paintings. I wondered that this should be my house, and thought, "Not bad". But then it occurred to me that I did not know what the lower floor looked like. Descending the stairs, I reached the ground floor. There everything was much older, and I realised that this part of the house must date from about the fifteenth or sixteenth century. The furnishings were mediaeval; the floors were of red brick. Everywhere it was rather dark. I went from one room to another, thinking, "Now I really must explore the whole house". I came upon a heavy door, and opened it. Beyond it, I discovered a stone stairway that lead down into the cellar. Descending again, I found myself in a beautifully vaulted room which looked exceedingly ancient. Examining the walls, I discovered layers of brick among the ordinary stone blocks, and chips of brick in the mortar. As soon as I saw this I knew that the walls dated from Roman times. My interest by now was intense. I looked more closely at the floor. It was on stone slabs, and in one of these I discovered a ring. When I pulled it, the stone slab lifted, and again I saw a stairway of narrow stone steps leading down into the depths. These, too, I descended, and entered a low cave cut into the rock. Thick dust lay on the floor, and in the dust were scattered bones and broken pottery, like remains of a primitive culture. I discovered two human skulls, obviously very old and half disintegrated. Then I awoke.'[5]

On board the *George Washington*, the three interpreted each other's dreams, though the traffic, it seems, was unequal, Freud being more willing to interpret than be interpreted.[6] According to Jung, Freud wished to stress an interpretation of his skull dream which centred on the idea of the death wish. Who, Freud asked, not unreasonably, did the skulls belong to? Jung says that he felt a strong intuitive resistance to this line of reasoning, but, reluctant to quarrel with Freud, lamely offered the suggestion that the skulls were those of his wife and sister-in-law. The real interpretation, he later confided to Aniela Jaffé, was more abstract:

'The ground floor stood for the first level of the unconscious. The deeper I went, the more alien and the darker the scene became. In the cave, I discovered remains of a primitive culture, that is, the world of the primitive man within myself – a world which can scarcely be reached or illuminated by consciousness. The primitive psyche of man borders on the life of the animal soul, just as the caves of prehistoric times were usually inhabited by animals before men laid claim to them. . . . My dream thus constituted a kind of structural diagram of the human psyche; it postulated something of an altogether *impersonal* nature underlying that psyche.'[7]

This disagreement had its antecedents. Earlier, before the ship had set sail, the three had enjoyed a lunch together in Bremen. It is Ernest Jones' assertion that Freud scored what he saw as a small victory over the younger Jung, persuading him, despite his normal abstemiousness, to drink wine. Having scored this triumph, Freud then fainted – and did so, Jones claims, because Freud identified Jung with his own younger brother who had died in infancy. Jung's recollection was different. Jung spoke at length over lunch, he later says, about the peat-bog corpses discovered in Northern Germany, prehistoric men drowned in the marshes or buried there, whose bodies were tanned by the bog's humic acid. Freud was well informed – better, in fact, than Jung – but he was 'inordinately vexed', and in the course of the conversation suddenly passed out. When he came round, Freud expressed himself convinced that 'all this chatter about corpses' meant that Jung had 'death-wishes towards him'. Jung says that he was surprised by this interpretation, and was alarmed by the intensity of Freud's fantasies – 'so strong, that, obviously, they could cause him to faint'.[8] So, when Jung dreamt of skulls on board the *George Washington*, and told Freud and Ferenczi what he had dreamt, the death wish was already an interpretative theme on Freud's mind. Was Freud on the right lines though? At this distance, one cannot arbitrate, but it is instructive to weigh certain possibilities.

Assume, for the present purpose, that the elements of Jung's dream are not in dispute: house, beautifully vaulted cellar and cave; secret staircase; two skulls and attendant bones; and the ambience of history rather than of the present day. If we may attribute a reading to Freud, it is one which homes in on the skulls, the bones and the cave construed as a tomb. Jung was not merely a young man preoccupied with death; he wished his mentor to die. Jung's reading is totally dissimilar. Like millions before and since, he uses ancient architecture as a metaphor of the mind and claims that consciousness is ordered layer on layer, like an archaeological dig.

Freud's reading is perfectly plausible, but it immediately reveals a vagueness over a centrally placed detail: the fact that there are two skulls, not one. Who might these belong to? Jung and Freud, perhaps? – in which case, they serve as a premonition: a warning to Jung of the death of their relationship, a possibility which he had doubtless sensed but had not yet acknowledged. Another possibility is that the skulls are those of Jung's parents. A dream in which an ambitious young man, in the course of a journey to the New World, kills off his parents would be by no means exceptional. In killing off parents and parent substitutes, he can become a parent of ideas in his own right.

A third possibility, perhaps the most attractive, is that the skulls belonged to just those people whom Jung had said they belonged to, his wife and sister-in-law – or, more exactly, to Freud's wife and sister-in-law – and, in the course either of dream or of recollection, were transposed. Consider Jung's position, and Freud's. Freud's seniority was at issue in the dangerous game of dream interpretation; but so too were more private anxieties. Jung seems to have known about these, perhaps on the basis of gossip; but Freud did not know that he knew. Freud's dreams on the *George Washington* bore, in Jung's view, on 'the triangle – Freud, his wife, and wife's younger sister'.[9] What that triangle in truth amounted to is still unclear; but it does seem that Freud was devoted to his sister-in-law as well as to his wife, and that they lived together in a state of domestic intimacy. Freud even took to holidaying with his clever sister-in-law Minna, leaving his wife Martha behind.

The nature of Freud's anxiety is explained by the ground plan of the flat at 19 Berggasse, in which Freud, Martha and Minna lived.[10] The master bedroom, in which Freud and Martha slept, has doors which open onto the living room, a walk-in cupboard, bathroom and water closet, a porch, and also onto Minna's bedroom. Minna's bedroom, on the other hand, could be reached only by going through the master bedroom. Her bedroom was an annexe of theirs. When Freud, Jung and Ferenczi were on the *George Washington*, Minna had been living with Martha and Freud for a year or so, and was then in her early forties. Her fiancé had recently died. Freud had abjured sexual relations with Martha for the past ten years or so. It was, without question, a tricky arrangement; more than enough to trouble a man's dreams.

What, from Jung's point of view, was the status of his remark to Freud about the identity of those two skulls? It might have been a piece of unconscious malice – paying Freud back for his refusal to act as an equal; the equivalent of a slip of the tongue. Or it might, on the other hand, have been an unconscious attempt at candour.

Floor Plan of Freud's Apartment

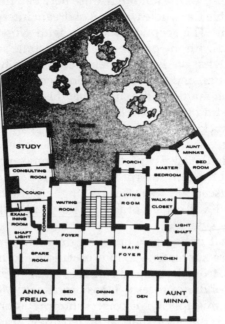

Adapted from Leupold-Löwenthal and Lobner (1975)

If he took pity on Freud's womenfolk, he was certainly not the last to do so.

In fact, there is no reason why several trains of thought could not have been in play simultaneously, nor why, as a result, several interpretations cannot coexist, all equally valid: why Jung should not have had a premonition of the death of his relationship with Freud, *and* have made a discovery of substance about the mind as organised like an archaeological dig, *and expressed* an intuitive insight into the nature of Freud's anxiety about Minna Bernays – all this without realising at the time what he had done. Nor is there any reason why, in making that remark to Freud about the skulls, his motives could not have been mixed. At such moments, motives often are. He could have been fobbing Freud off, *and* attempting candour, *and* mounting a spiteful if glancing attack.

39

Disagreements of the kind that arose between Jung and Freud make vulnerable the whole tradition of dream interpretation that they represent. The sceptical scientist, with work to do in his laboratory and with the prospect of adding some small but solid increment to what we know is tempted to turn his back on all such endeavours, and to pour scorn on them for good measure. The next chapter outlines the shape that this radical attack on the interpretative tradition takes. Before moving on, though, it is as well to take stock: the picture, I want to suggest, may be murky but is by no means as black as it can be made to seem. Part of the difficulty lies in the false expectations that some exponents of the old tradition of dream interpretation fostered; namely, that all dreams are susceptible to a clear reading, and that this reading, when achieved, will consist of a single story rather than of several stories side by side.

The idea that only a proportion of dreams, perhaps a small proportion, are susceptible to interpretation – to translation, in Freud's terms, from the ground-rules of primary-process thought to those of secondary-process – is easily grasped. More difficult is the idea of a multiplicity of correct interpretations; and more difficult still is the idea that, although they appear mutually exclusive, they can nonetheless lock together in formally satisfactory patterns. However, these notions are important to what follows, and especially to the discussion of systematic ambiguity in Chapter 7.

Dreams like Jung's on the *George Washington* of the two skulls are patently complex. Semantically, they are multifaceted, conveying not one meaning but several meanings that may or may not be related. The dream itself can be represented as an octagonal cell with dotted lines:[11]

Interpretations are often multifaceted too. And while each will normally have a bearing on the dream, they often have nothing in common one with the other – as was the case with Freud's interpretation of the skulls and Jung's:

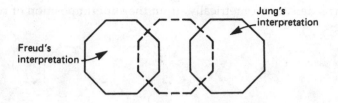

As René Thom the geometer says, 'In no case has mathematics any right to dictate anything to reality.'[12] Nevertheless, it can create expectations in the investigator's mind, and provide him too with a repertoire of formal categories and distinctions that he might otherwise lack. In the present case, cell diagrams have formal properties that are otherwise by no means easy to see. One notes, for example, that when new interpretations are introduced, although quite different from those already in place, they can serve to knit the diagram as a whole into a coherent pattern:

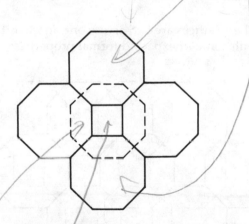

Although excessively tidy, perhaps, these diagrams also have hidden resources. While, here, the four interpretative cells overlap the dream cell, the one drawn in dotted lines, they do not cover it completely. By implication, in other words, there is an area of strangeness at the heart of the dream that waking thought, however ingenious, leaves untouched: in Freud's phrase, the dream's 'navel', its point of contact with the unknown. It is worth reflecting, too, that these octagonal cell patterns derive, geometrically, from the superimposition of two lattices:

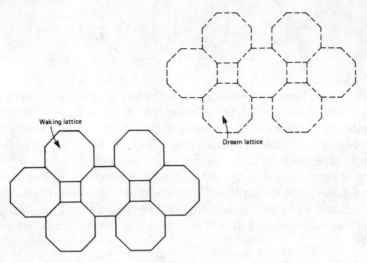

When these lattices are laid across one another, there results a pattern with some unexpected formal properties:

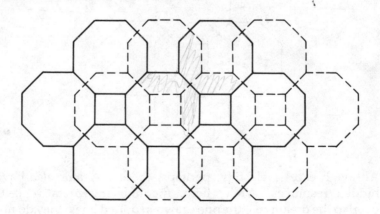

If you read the pattern in terms of the solid lines, the waking lattice, each cell now has an internal structure made up of dotted lines, ones that are part of the dream lattice. If you read the pattern in terms of the dotted lines, the dream lattice, each cell has an internal structure made up of solid lines – from the waking lattice:

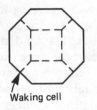

Waking cell

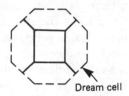

Dream cell

The implication, in other words, is that while our waking thoughts have an internal structure that is dream-like, our dreams have an internal structure that has the properties of waking thought: that there is an intimate reciprocity between the sleeping and waking modes. In a way more surprising still is a hint provided by such diagrams about the relation between cells, whether waking or dreaming. For although each cell in the waking lattice shares its boundaries with other cells, and similarly each cell in the dreaming lattice, overlap or communality between cells is only achieved by moving from one lattice to the other:

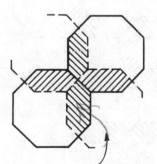

Communality between waking cells

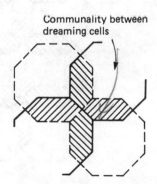

Communality between dreaming cells

This suggests that our transition from one idea or body of ideas within our waking thought is always dependent on processes that are dream-like; movement from one dream to another can only be achieved by means that are those of waking thought. It is in this intimate interdependence that the solution to the problem posed at the end of the last chapter surely lies. The tendency of interpretative argument to tame or domesticate the antic properties of the dream, correctly identified by Lacan as a fault in orthodox psychoanalysis, is removed. The fabric of systematic interpretation – and, by implication, of the natural sciences too – is as dependent on the intuitive leap, these diagrams suggest, as the dream is upon the patiently constructed network of interpretation. The idea that knowledge can grow by means of wholly explicit rules is as much a fiction as the idea that dreams have meanings that can be left to speak for themselves.

A fabric of interpretative argument, considered as whole, will then have the following form:

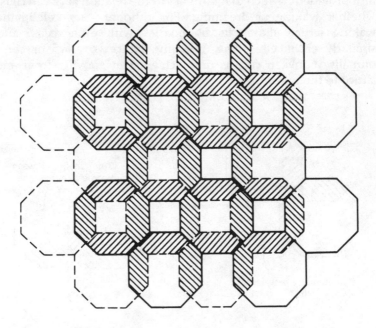

This diagram stands as a rough-and-ready summary or caricature of the assumptions about interpretative argument on which the rest of this book is based, whether applied to the dream or to texts that are more durable. It depends on tensions between the intuitive and the analytic, the metaphorical and the literal; it is ordered and disciplined, but conglomerate in form rather than neat and bounded; and it contains windows of mystery, where overlap between the intuitive and analytic, metaphorical and literal, cannot be achieved.[13]

A further moral of such diagrams is their exclusion of the 'muscular' approach. In search of a simple explanation, the interpreter is often tempted to reach through the filigree of argument and grasp the 'realities' that lie behind it; to neglect the manifest in order to grasp laws that are hidden. Arguably, such gestures can succeed in science and technology. A welter of evidence can be brought to heel by means of laws that, once imposed, seem delightfully simple – and it is in just this movement from the apparently chaotic to the simple that the aesthetic appeal of science is often thought to lie. In the arts, on the other hand, it is characteristically the role of the artist not so much to invent or impose as to reveal: to pierce the veils of false consciousness and self-deception with which our experience is shrouded. And when one comes to the meanings of dreams, these diagrams imply, the least hint of grasping muscularity dooms the venture. In interpretative or 'hermeneutic' work, whether applied to dreams or to more public texts and signs, one advances not by reference to explanatory theories that are extraneous to the text, but by fastidious respect for what the text says. If the hermeneut is impatient of its fine grain, the progress he makes will be illusory.

Notes

(1) Jung (1964), p. 29. Jung's method was that of controlled or directed association.
(2) Quoted by Roazen (1975), p. 268.
(3) Jung (1983), p. 26.
(4) Brome (1978), p. 33.
(5) Jung (1983), p. 182.
(6) Jones reports Jung as saying that 'Freud's dreams seemed to

be mostly concerned with cares for the future of his family and of his work': Jones (1961), p. 266. Jung, on the other hand, recalls an altogether more emotionally fraught exchange. Freud responded to his interpretation with 'a look of the utmost suspicion', and then said, 'But I cannot risk my authority.' This Jung saw as a turning-point in their relationship: Jung (1983), p. 181.

(7) Jung (1983), p. 184.

(8) Ibid., p. 179. A number of sources bear on this episode. Jones discusses it, although his views are so partisan as to be virtually worthless: see e.g. Sulloway (1979), pp. 480–4. Brome (1978) devotes the bulk of a chapter to it, and Roazen (1975) examines it too. Freud fainted twice in Jung's presence; on this occasion, in 1909, when the tension between them was first surfacing, and again in 1912 when the split between them was irreparable. Jung, in later life, was contemptuous: Freud 'could not stand a critical word. . . . Just like a woman. Confront her with a disagreeable truth: she faints.' Why, though, did Freud, who disliked 'the faint mental obfuscation that even a slight drink induces', wish the abstemious Jung to drink wine with himself and Ferenczi? The answer, Roazen suggests, might lie in Freud's desire to shift Jung's allegiance from Bleuler, who insisted on complete abstinence, towards himself and Ferenczi: Roazen (1975), p. 246.

(9) Roazen (1975), p. 246.

(10) The role of architecture as a format for psychic states is an issue opened by Frances Yates' remarkable book *The Art of Memory* (1969). In ancient times, buildings were used as mnemonic aids, with ideas, figuratively speaking, being put in various rooms. Nowadays, they are stored in memoranda. Even so, we may still need architecture as an aid: for instance, in unpacking the metaphors of which our explanations consist – witness the use of the cinema as a metaphor in Chapter 11.

(11) I have used these octagonal patterns and lattices elsewhere: Hudson (1975). Their properties are formal, of course. They are no more tied to a particular subject-matter than is the correlation coefficient or are metaphors like the field, boundary or path. Closely adjacent, there stands the beauti-

ful edifice of Thom and Zeeman's catastrophe theory. It is tempting to borrow its elegance and authority but, for the time being at least, this would be a mistake. What the study of the dream at present needs are the simple virtues of cottage geometry. The cell pattern used here, incidentally, is one that quilt-makers call 'square and church window'.

(12) Woodcock and Davis (1980), p. 77.

(13) Jung's interest in mandalas, though superficially similar, was more personal: 'My mandalas were cryptograms concerning the state of the self which were presented to me anew each day. In them I saw the self – that is, my whole being – actively at work. To be sure, at first I could only dimly understand them; but they seemed to me highly significant, and I guarded them like precious pearls. . . . The self, I thought, was like the monad which I am, and which is my world. The mandala represents this monad, and corresponds to the microcosmic nature of the psyche': Storr (1983), p. 234.

CHAPTER FIVE

Science's Counter-Blast

At the very moment when Freud and Jung were at odds with one another on the *George Washington*, an altogether more forthright approach to the problem of dreams and their meanings was taking shape. The early years of the century saw not only the establishment of psychoanalysis as an identifiable – if internally fissured – body of thought, but also the birth of an antagonistic system of belief among psychologists: behaviourism.

Nowadays, in scientific circles, both Freud and Jung are usually dismissed, even-handedly, as 'unscientific' – the implication being not that they were artists, or scholars, worthy enough conditions in their own ways, but that they were purveyors of irrationality, superstition. This dismissal has several justifications, some philosophical or conceptual in nature, others more a matter of fact. Taken together, these constitute what might be called the 'scientific attitude', now dominant in academic departments of psychology throughout the Anglo-Saxon world. It is a state of mind that occasionally presents itself as an explicit system of beliefs about the nature of knowledge, but takes the form, characteristically, of slackly articulated prejudices about the sorts of psychology that are respectable and the sorts that are not.

The most sweepingly uncompromising are the philosophical objections. These amount, in practice, to the claim that dreams are an irrelevance and can safely be ignored. Any one of at least four attitudes may be adopted, although these are often jumbled promiscuously together and confused. The first is 'epiphenomenalism' – the belief that all events in the mind are by-products of events in the brain. The second is 'behaviourism', as narrowly defined – the belief that events in the mind, being hidden from the impartial observer's view, cannot be the proper subject-matter of science. The third is 'materialism' – the belief that mental events, including, presumably, materialistic beliefs themselves, do not exist. The fourth is 'positivism' – the influential but strangely arbitrary doctrine that there can be only two kinds of knowledge: propositions that are questions of publicly ascertainable fact, and propositions that are true by definition, like those of mathematics. All other propositions are meaningless, in just the way that a sneeze or belch is.

Such ideas have parts to play in the games that professional philosophers play with one another for their mutual benefit or irritation, and as such are harmless. Difficulties arise, though, when they are exported to neighbouring disciplines such as psychology. Sometimes, it is true, they act as a stimulant. Epiphenomenalism, for example, popular among psychology students in the 1950s and 1960s, is now in vogue among sociologists. Where once all mental states, including dreams, were assumed to be irrelevant because they were by-products of brain states, they are now assumed to be irrelevant because they are by-products of processes that are social, cultural. Recently, I have seen a sophisticated Ph.D. thesis in the making, in which it was taken for granted that dreams become real only in being spoken about, and that, even then, there is nothing more to them than what is said. Apparently capricious, a species of literary conceit, the effect was interesting, in that it focused attention on an aspect of the dream often overlooked – the ways in which it is used in conversation.

More often the consequences are mischievous. In British psychology, epiphenomenalism has served as a part of the rationale for a sustained programme of mind-bending. Without foundation in fact or logic, this has distorted the subject's growth, stifling work on the more complex aspects of human nature, largely by channelling the talented and energetic in other directions, and protecting laboratory research from the criticism it needs if it is to thrive.[1]

One of the curiosities of the use made of philosophical beliefs in psychology – epiphenomenalism, behaviourism, materialism, positivism, whether in old or new-fangled forms – is that while they appear tough-minded and scientific, they are almost invariably advanced without reference to evidence. Their truth, in other words, is assumed to be self-evident. As such, we are at liberty to pick them up or put them down as they suit our needs. They may attract, but they by no means compel. My own inclination is to leave them alone.

Of far greater concern is the next sort of objection. This is conceptual rather than genuinely philosophical in character, and consists in the complaint that Freud's dream theory, and psychoanalytic argument more generally, proves in practice to be too elastic. Such theory is used to accommodate any item of evidence advanced against it, however damning. This rubberiness is seen as a fatal flaw: proof that Freud and his cohorts belong to the realm not of science but of superstition.

Many theories, models and metaphors in and around science are rubbery too, of course, in that they make all-embracing and sometimes startling claims but at the same time give no indication of how they could be disproved: the notion, for example, that the brain can be treated as an information-processing system. Darwin's theory of natural selection, to take a weightier instance, has held sway for more than a century, not because it has been subjected to an exacting series of experimental tests, but because it accommodates most of the pertinent evidence we possess, because it is parsimonious, and because no one has yet thought of a convincing alternative.[2]

If psychoanalytic theory has much in common with other theories, uneasiness nonetheless lingers. In the face of the apparently unresolvable disagreements that arise between analysts confronted with the same dream or neurotic symptom, it is clearly unacceptable to assume that the activity as a whole is as unproblematic as, say, research in organic chemistry.[3] It is not acceptable, for example, to claim, as a matter of established fact, that salt in dreams always stands for semen, or ink for faeces. One can quite easily picture a dream in which such an interpretation was justified by its context, and was seen as persuasive by all parties, the dreamer among them. But the claim to possess a master key that unlocks all doors, all dreams, is mistaken. Locks differ, and so do dreams. In some dreams, salt may stand for semen, and ink for faeces, but in others such a reading may be far-fetched, and in yet more an irrelevance. Each lock is picked on its merits. Thus it is not just that dream interpretations can stand in complex relations to one another, several equally persuasive interpretative stories coexisting, nor even that the margins of reasonable doubt in dream interpretation are larger than those habitually met with in science (though not larger, one would have thought, than those accepted as a matter of routine in, say, cosmology). It is that, as is standard practice in the critical and scholarly arts, biography and detective work, but uncommon in science, each interpretation focuses upon the particular.

At least in detail, each individual's dream life is unique. It will almost certainly embody familiar motifs and themes, but in its fine grain it is like no other. It is also unique in that its interpretative context is the experience of the dreamer. In the dispute between Jung and Freud over Jung's dream of the two skulls, an interpretation's reference is not to some over-arching theory, but to the systems of meaning locked inside Jung's head, and to the waking context in which he was immersed. Dream interpretation does not test a hypothesis, as experiments in laboratory science are expected to. It seeks to accommodate evidence, much as explanations do in a natural science like palaeontology, say. It is an attempt to make sense of an apparently puzzling episode in a given individual's life.[4]

To admit that dream interpretation differs from science is not to concede that it must be slovenly. On the contrary, it is to point to forms of rigour that differ from those found in most forms of natural and experimental science, but that are in principle no less public or codifiable. Implicitly, it is to claim for dream interpretation, and for the interpretative aspects of psychology more generally, a place on the map of disciplines that is neither among the arts nor among the sciences, but somewhere in the mid-ground, with the natural sciences as neighbours on one side and activities like biography, history and criticism as neighbours on the other.[5]

In short, while anxieties over the elasticity of orthodox psycho-analytic theories of the dream are justified, they are not grounds for despair. Certainly, they do not exclude forms of dream interpretation that are more circumspect.

The remaining objection to the psychoanalytic tradition is more nearly factual, and it is here that excitement at present arises. The suggestion is that Freud, and those like him, got the wrong end of the stick: that they misunderstood what the brain is *for*, what its purpose is. The mind, such critics assert, is a system for generating and testing meanings; one which, for eight hours each night, regularly slips out of gear. The meanings which pass through the mind when it is out of gear, when its owners are asleep, are largely or completely random; a semantic salad. One might as well look for the meanings of dreams as try to reconstruct the pattern of a Fair Isle sweater from its yarn once it has been unravelled. This thrust, aimed at the heart of the psychoanalytic theory, has been prepared with some care, and it draws support from the massive growth of research in the sleep laboratory.

The discovery that dreams are associated in human beings with the physiological phenomenon of the REM or 'rapid eye movement' phase of sleep, though important in itself, is not damaging to the psychoanalytic cause. Dreaming, it seems, occurs throughout the night, but is associated particularly with this phase of the sleep cycle; one characterised by flickering movements of the eyes, by exceptionally low muscle tone, around the head and neck especially, and by a pattern of electrical activity on the brain's surface reminiscent of someone lying awake with his eyes shut.[6]

Much more disconcerting is the discovery that REM sleep is a feature of the lives of all viviparous mammals, not all of whom can sensibly be assumed to have repressed wishes. REM sleep has been observed in all placental and marsupial species so far studied; is a brief but detectable feature of the sleep of birds; and is found in modified form in some reptiles. The mole and opossum have roughly the same amount of REM sleep, proportionally, as human adults do.[7] Just as telling is the discovery that human beings display REM sleep as new-born babies – and even, it seems, while still in the womb. Roughly half the new-born human infant's sleep is spent in the REM phase, this proportion dropping steadily with age until, in adulthood, the proportion is as low as 15 per cent, the opposite of what one would predict if Freud were right and dreams expressed repressed wishes.

More worrying still, if one seeks to defend the traditional view, is the evidence that, during REM sleep, the cerebral cortex comes under the control of the brain's lower centres, powerful and apparently non-specific signals passing up from the brain stem to the cerebral cortex, subjecting it to what has been called 'a varied pattern of bangs' – a stimulation that is apparently quite random.[8] The obvious implication of this physiological evidence is that dreams are the by-products of powerful biological forces, and that any painstaking attempt to unravel their contents rests on a mistake – not of philosophical principle, now, but of demonstrable scientific fact.

This 'brain stem' or 'bottom-up' view of dreaming has proved hugely attractive. At a stroke, it cuts away broad acres of tortured argument about the dream-work and unconscious fantasy, much as the positivistic revolution in the philosophy of the 1930s cut away neo-Hegelian metaphysics. As an intellectual manoeuvre, it is exhilarating, creating at least the illusion of fresh air to breathe.

However, it faces difficulties of its own. Chief among them is the claim, made by a very large number of intelligent and sophisticated observers, that while many dreams may well be random, a significant proportion do indeed have meanings; ones that, when subjected to the minimum of unscrambling, can be shown to bear on the dreamer's waking experience. At the most straightforward of levels, the dream may echo vivid experience directly. A person who, fifteen years before, emerged from a Nazi concentration camp, may still suffer nightmares: SS guards who persecute, 'selections' in which he waits to be chosen and sent to his death. The tension seems unbearable and the individual is woken either by his own screams or by those of fellow inmates.[9]

Here, the connection with waking experience is obvious. It can also be more subtle. A woman may claim that she dreams repeatedly of escaping from concentration camps, although she has never herself been in one. She describes in detail the dream's recurring features: the feeling of panic, the barbed wire and searchlights, the sound of the dogs barking in the distance, panting as they grow closer. She too may tell of the terror in which she awakes, her pulse racing and her nightdress soaked in sweat, and of the fear she experiences afterwards in going back to sleep.

There is a tendency among the experimentally inclined either to ignore such testimony, or to shelve it on the assumption that it will fall into place once a theory of more ordinary dreams is securely in place. Plainly, one can do neither. It is wise, certainly, to be cautious, taking note of the way a dream like this is told, watchful for signs of theatricality. But to assume that such experience is meaningless precludes further questions which can legitimately be raised. It may occur to the dreamer, for instance, that 'escape' dreams have plagued her in the past; and have done so, she now realises, whenever she has felt trapped within an intimate relationship. As she dwells on this insight, it may also occur to her that there are significant details of the dream that she has in the past lacked the courage to identify: that the sound of the dogs' breath, say, is not only terrifying but reminiscent of certain unwelcome sorts of sexual intimacy. And this realisation, in its turn, may give her, vividly, the sense of a crisis survived. It is not just a skein of sense that interpretation establishes in such an instance, interpretation for interpretation's sake, but a fuller awareness on the dreamer's part of the nature of her own experience.

'Bottom-up' theory can of course be patched, and there are both old-fashioned and more up-to-date ways of attempting this. In the manner of the 1960s, now rather old-hat, one can envisage the brain's memory as though it were a library, and waking access to that library as dependent on its filing system. We are free to browse but, whenever the need arises, the filing system is the principle to which we revert. Sleeping access, in contrast, can be seen as random, in that it is governed by principles that have nothing to do with the books' contents: the colours, say, of the books' bindings, or their size. The output of this nocturnal access has as little coherent meaning as pebbles on a beach or patterns of sunlight in leaves.[10]

This output can nonetheless be scanned for meaning, especially perhaps in the case of those dreams that occur just before the individual wakes up. The sense-seeking centres of the brain might be seen as switching on just before the transition from the sleeping to waking state is made, the retrieval system thus favouring those dreams in which the semblance of meaning is present. The system might further be tightened by placing a magical synthesiser in the library basement, which not merely conglomerates memories (putting together a familiar face, say, with an inappropriate name; a familiar nose with an inappropriate moustache), but smoothes these discrepant elements into people, objects and situations that are genuinely new. In making such adaptations to the 'bottom-up' view of dreaming, however, one spoils the economy of the original conception, and one does so on the basis of mechanisms – the magical synthesiser in the basement, for instance – for which there is as yet no compelling anatomical, physiological or chemical rationale.

In recent years, this kind of theorising about the dream has had a new impetus in the form of the analogy with the computer. The dreaming brain, it has been pointed out, is strongly reminiscent of a computer in its 'off-line' state. Active, but without input or output, it is well placed to perform its necessary domestic functions. Various suggestions have been made about what these domestic functions might amount to.[11]

More ingenious are arguments based not on the computer as such but on models constructed on the principle of the associative network. Rather than aiming to achieve the optimal efficiency in memory storage or calculation, these more closely mimic the brain, and are designed to learn, remember or discriminate in much the way that the brain does. These models usually exist as computer programs, but one at least has taken solid form: Aleksander's robot Wisard. With the aid of a television camera, this learns to discriminate, as the brain does, between closely related visual patterns: to tell, for example, whether the person sitting in front of it is smiling or frowning.[12] It is certainly Aleksander's view that dreaming can occur within such networks as they 'relax': that is to say, as they are temporarily released from the control that the external environment exerts upon them, and freewheel back towards a neutral state. In the language of automata theory, dream thought is thus a 'trajectory' through a 'state space': a route back through all those other trajectories that the network has established while under external environmental control.

Crick and Mitchison have used another model in the same family to sustain a different view of why dreams occur. They argue that the brain dreams in order to forget. In the course of normal growth and everyday experience, they believe, the brain is bound to generate 'parasitic' patterns of response: thought patterns that are useless or positively maladaptive, and that serve to overload it. Somehow these must be shed; and it is this function that REM sleep performs. The brain stem bombards the cerebral cortex with the random bangs that 'damp down' or 'tune out' the network's undesirable links.[13]

The development of such networks is in its earliest and most exploratory phase, and their relation to the explanation of dreaming is still a matter of conjecture. While the characteristics of the dream – the processes of condensation and displacement observed by Freud, for instance – can be discussed in a general way as 'emergent properties' of these networks, there is no guarantee that in practice they are going to provide the basis of an adequate explanation. Meanwhile, each theory has its snags, and Crick and Mitchison's, despite its elegance and originality, has several. The first it shares with Freud's. It is exceptionally difficult to see how it could be proved either right or wrong. To show that it is right, as the authors themselves acknowledge, one would have to demonstrate that the occurrence of a forgotten dream reduces the dreamer's chances of having that dream again – a task of verification that boggles the imagination. It is Crick's belief that in the face of such a conundrum, psychological methods are bound to be inconclusive, and that the best hope of a decisive outcome lies in the study of the biochemistry of synaptic connections within the brain – and, in this, he echoes Freud, who observed that the deficiencies of the psychoanalytic description of the mind 'would probably vanish if we were already in a position to replace the psychological terms by physiological or chemical ones'.[14]

A second snag is the implication that the recollection of dreams is a bad thing, its effect being to overload the system and reduce the efficiency with which the recalling individual thinks. The clear prediction of the Crick and Mitchison theory is that habitual recallers will prove more addled in their wits than non-recallers, but the evidence seems to contradict this. Nor are there clear signs that the suppression of REM sleep by means of drugs muddles waking thought or distorts our powers of memory, though the theory leads one to expect that this will be so.[15]

Speaking more technically, the particular network model they espouse has a number of controversial features. Arguably, certain of the assumptions embodied in the net's design are worryingly arbitrary. More generally, there is doubt about whether this highly idealised model or any of its immediate rivals quite meet their central design requirement. For if associative networks are to be convincingly brain-like, they must strike a delicate balance. They must be geared to events in the external world, not merely echoing or shadowing environmental changes in a passive way, but predicting them. To do this successfully, however, they must also have the freedom, figuratively, to step back from the pressure the environment exerts – to organise their own knowledge, and be in a position to impose orders on the external world that are novel. In other words, they must be intimately responsive to external stimuli, but at the same time have the power to form their own intentions and see these through to effective action. The model Crick and Mitchison adopt seems, to some eyes, to cope with neither of these essentially brain-like functions entirely persuasively. On the other hand, it does accord a central role to the activity of the brain stem during REM sleep, a strong point in its favour, whereas 'relaxation' theories take no special account of it.

While there is no incompatibility between the 'relaxation' view of the dream adopted by Aleksander and the assumption that dreams have interpretable meanings, the Crick and Mitchison theory seems at first sight directly antagonistic to such an assumption. Dreams, in their account, rather than being express-ions of unconscious wishes or glimpses of some more compre-hensive imaginative fabric, are the equivalent of household rubbish, detritus to be swept away. But in fact, Crick's view proves unexpectedly cautious:

'We think it unlikely that remembering dreams will do much harm unless carried to great excess. An analogy with blood letting might help. This, like Freudian analysis, was at one time a favourite medical treatment, though there is no evidence that it did good and some that it caused harm. Yet we would all agree that taking a *small* sample of blood for diagnostic purposes is useful. In the same way, if really useful infor-mation about a person can be obtained from dreams, and not in any other way, it would be sensible to remember them and have them analysed. I would go further and say that eventually I expect a really scientific method of analysing dreams to emerge, but perhaps not in this century.'[16]

Having threatened root-and-branch annihilation not only of psychoanalytic theory, but of any attempt to make sense of the dream's contents, 'bottom-up' theory is here seen, if not in a positively welcoming guise, at least in one of tolerant catholicity.

'Bottom-up' theorising about the dream still faces a problem of method, however, and it is only when this is overcome that the nature of the conjunction between brain research and dream interpretation will become more nearly clear. If network models of the brain are to be used in explaining the dream, they must be geared to detailed analyses of the formal properties that the dream in fact possesses. Artificial intelligence must be geared to natural history. Once these analyses are in being, the performance of the various network models can be demonstrated step by step, and their strengths and weaknesses compared. Until then, we are stuck in the phase of the spirited hypothesis and airy conjecture.

One item in such analyses will be the fact that dreams, like fantasies and intuitions, are sometimes linked in a useful way to their owner's deliberative thought. The brain is capable, as Crick and Mitchison say, 'of learning very large amounts of novel information'. It can also solve problems. Without stating this explicitly, Crick and Mitchison suggest that the brain does this by assimilating novel information to interpretative patterns, plans, hypotheses, schemes or 'schemata' that already exist, or that evolve gradually in the light of experience. The evidence of psychological research, though, whether on visual perception or everyday judgement, problem-solving or originality, is that more is afoot. [17] The brain can switch from one schema to another quite abruptly; and it can create new schemata by engaging in what Einstein called combinatory or associative play. [18]

When Einstein remarked, as he is said to have done, that the scientist with the capacity for original thought is the one with access to his dreams, he did not mean that the solutions to their problems come to scientists as a matter of course while they are asleep, though this does sometimes happen. Rather, that it is in combinatory play between 'psychical entities', between certain 'signs and more or less clear images', that the essential feature of productive thought lies. This combinatory play, he insisted, was prior to, and clearly distinguishable from, the expression of relationships between ideas that are publicly intelligible. He was also insistent, incidentally, that words or language, 'as they are written or spoken', played no role in his mechanism of thought.

When struggling to make sense, the brain needs rudiments on which to work, raw materials from which a new pattern can be built. Some will come from public sources, books, the media, teachers, friends. Some will be transposed from one topic to another; a matter of internal transfer. But some, it seems plain, emerge from information previously rejected as irrelevant, but nonetheless held in store. The brain, to put the same point in another way, will in certain contexts function most effectively if it is free to glean useful items from among those classified for the time being as irrelevant or parasitic. It is this activity, the creation of a new order from elements discarded by a current one, that a model like Crick and Mitchison's should accommodate; and it can do so, it seems, only if it is elaborated.

Apposite is the metaphor not of domestic rubbish but of the bric-à-brac stall. Every day, all around us, households in which each object had its place are broken up, and the possessions in question dispersed. The value of dispersed objects is not always obvious, hence the bric-à-brac stall. On this are jumbled together a few objects that may be of real value with the many that are virtually but not quite useless: the tarnished caddy spoon that might have been silver, the begrimed oil painting that looks vaguely genuine. Most of the stall's objects will be glanced at by its customers in passing and ignored. A few will prove to have a definite but limited value. Only a tiny minority will be treasures, having the magnetic allure that lends direction to their hunters' lives. A special virtue of this bric-à-brac analogy is that it admits individual differences. Each customer can be allowed his own style; some scrupulously blinkered and collecting only one type of object, others allowing chance discoveries to trigger one new enthusiasm after another. Some collect as an idle habit, others as a consuming passion. Others still, it must be said, do not collect second-hand goods at all, and buy nothing that is not brand new. The relation of the dream to waking thought, as I shall hope to show later, is not only one in which human beings display their variety, but one in which that variety is turned to good account.

Having threatened a complete demolition of established beliefs about the dream, the critique derived from the sleep laboratory and the computer seems to be settling, for the time being at least, upon a position of surprising moderation.[19] The rhythmic bangs emanating from the brain stem during REM sleep remain of importance, and so does evidence about REM sleep in new-born infants and in the mammalian world at large. Beguiling, too, are the properties of models based on the idea of the neural network. In evolutionary terms sleep and dreaming still present a puzzle, however. As Rechtschaffen says:

> 'If sleep does not serve an absolutely vital function, then it is the biggest mistake the evolutionary process has ever made. Sleep precludes hunting for and consuming food. It is incompatible with procreation. It produces vulnerability to attack from enemies. . . . How could sleep have remained virtually unchanged as a monstrously useless, maladaptive vestige throughout the whole of mammalian evolution while selection has during the same period of time been able to achieve all kinds of delicate, finely-tuned adjustments in the shape of fingers and toes?'[20]

This evolutionary puzzle and the question of the brain's operating principles are tied together, as Crick and Mitchison correctly assume. What they do not entertain is the possibility of an altogether more sweepingly synthetic and at the same time more rigorous explanation, in which these biological considerations are gathered together with another more strictly psychological one: the question of the formal properties implicit in the meanings of dreams themselves. In such a synthesis, 'bottom-up' and 'top-down' theorising about the sleeping brain and its products would knit together, and the conceptual gap within psychology between mechanistic and interpretative modes of explanation would close. Associative network models of the brain could be fashioned to mimic the forms of thought that dreams as a matter of fact display: not merely their ambiguity, as the chapters which follow show, but the compatibility of ambiguous meanings with a strong sense of design, and the possibility too that such designs permit an unambiguous resolution. Such a synthesis is as exciting a prospect as any that psychology now offers, and eminently achievable – although at present it hovers in the mid-distance, still out of reach.

Despite the élan of laboratory-based theories about the dream, it is a world in which, to date, less has changed than at first seems likely. A hundred years ago, in *The Descent of Man*, Darwin found it natural to connect the topics of the dream and the imagination. He concludes that 'The value of the products of our imagination depends of course on the number, accuracy, and clearness of our impressions, on our judgement and taste in selecting or rejecting the involuntary combinations, and to a certain extent on our power of voluntarily combining them.' He goes on to assume that human beings can in this respect be discussed on equal terms with other species: 'As dogs, cats, horses, and probably all the higher animals, even birds have vivid dreams, and this is shown by their movements and the sounds uttered, we must admit that they possess some power of imagination.'[21]

This seems as good a foundation as any on which to build an argument that synthesises, and that takes as its centre the intimacy of the link between the dream and the imagination.

Notes

(1) Hudson (1972) and in press.

(2) Darwin's notion of the survival of the fittest is now being supplemented (but not displaced) by others: 'genetic drift', for example, and, more recently, 'molecular drive'.

(3) See, e.g., Latour and Woolgar (1979), especially their chapter on the steps whereby Guillemin and Schally's discovery of TRF, or thyrotropin releasing factor, came to be established as the fact for which they were jointly awarded the Nobel Prize.

(4) Appositely, Rycroft insists that he has 'no wish to lumber the world with yet another theory of dreams': Rycroft (1979), p. 168. Dreams 'are best understood', he says, 'even in a clinical setting, if one forgets all theories about them and ceases to think of them as discrete phenomena or items of experience, but instead responds to them as glimpses of the dreamer's total imaginative fabric'.

(5) Such maps are not easy to draw. Academic psychologists habitually speak as if there were only one relevant dimension: hard, which equals 'scientific', and soft, which encompasses a messy brew of superstition, persuasion and entertainment. Any such formulation overlooks the existence of technology as a separate estate, and the existence, too, of technologies like photography that are also art-forms. It ignores such scholarly arts as history, except in as much as they can be made to look like proto-sciences, and ignores the rigours that are an essential element of all art-forms and that are especially apparent in music.

(6) Oswald (1980) offers an authoritative introduction to the physiology of sleep and dreaming; Cohen (1979) is one of several books offering more detailed coverage of the material relevant to the psychologist. The biology of sleep is highly complex. There is evidence, for example, that while the brain is asleep its biochemical imbalances are restored. More interesting to the psychologist is the discovery that, during REM, the male of the species almost always has an erection; infants, adults and the old alike. Oswald observes, in explanation, that the regions of the brain controlling REM sleep 'are the powerhouses for other primitive forms of behaviour, including emotional expression and mating activity': Oswald (1980), p. 84.

(7) The adult spiny anteater, as Crick and Mitchison (1983) note with interest, appears to have no REM sleep. The explanation may lie in its exceptionally large brain; an evolutionary cul-de-sac, they suggest, a design that just did not work.

(8) Ibid.

(9) Oswald (1980), p. 90. He cites the work of Eitinger, who studied the dreams of 600 survivors of the Nazi concentration camps, fifteen years on.

(10) Waking and sleeping access, it is tempting to suggest, reflects some special involvement of the left and right cerebral hemispheres respectively. Cohen's (1979) is one of many voices counselling caution, however. As Foulkes (1978) points out, dreams characteristically involve an integration of the verbal with the visual, the sequential with the non-sequential. Dreams are said to cease not only after damage to the right hemisphere, but after damage to parts of the left hemisphere mediating language, and after the disconnection of one hemisphere from the other.

(11) See Evans (1983).

(12) Aleksander (1983).

(13) Crick and Mitchison (1983). Their theory was developed in parallel with a more mathematical treatment of the same issue by Hopfield and his colleagues (1983). I am indebted to Dr Crick for his comments on an earlier version of this chapter, which was in important respects confused. I am also very much in Professor Aleksander's debt for his advice and help.

(14) Crick, personal communication, 22 May 1984; Freud in *Beyond the Pleasure Principle*, quoted by Sulloway (1979), p. 126.

(15) A troublesome feature of Crick and Mitchison's exposition is their assumption that dreams are 'unconscious' if they are not recalled. The likelihood is that, while asleep, we are vividly aware of many dreams, only a tiny minority of which are recalled. Whether it is waking recall or sleeping consciousness that prevents 'parasitic' information from being shed is not quite clear. In either case, it is a little surprising that, in the course of its evolution, the brain should not have lost this design fault altogether.

(16) Crick, personal communication, 22 May 1984.

(17) Bartlett (1932), Craik (1943), Gregory (1966) have all adopted this point of view.

(18) Quoted by Hadamard (1945), p. 142.

(19) The division between the sleep laboratory and psycho-analysis is not always as sharp as this chapter might be seen to imply. In the United States, especially, impressively sustained attempts have been made to knit the two worlds together: notably Foulkes's book *The Grammar of Dreams* (1978), and Pribram and Gill's (1976) reanalysis of Freud's *Project*.

(20) Rechtschaffen (1971), quoted by Cohen (1979), p. 24. The usual reaction to this evolutionary puzzle is that, while asleep, the brain must perform some essential restorative function, rectifying imbalances in the brain created when the animal is awake. The evidence suggests that such restorative functions are indeed performed, but that they occur predominantly during non-REM sleep.

(21) Darwin (1887), p. 74.

CHAPTER SIX

Dreams and the Literary Imagination

In *The Descent of Man*, Darwin sandwiches his section on the 'Imagination', appropriately enough, between others on 'Memory' and 'Reason'. Earlier in the same passage, he borrows a phrase from the German romantic poet Jean Paul Richter. Recently, this phrase has been recognised as important by Charles Rycroft, and it is going to serve here as the hinge on which my own argument turns.

By means of the imagination, Darwin argues, man 'unites former images and ideas, independently of the will, and thus creates brilliant and novel results'. It is in the dream that we get the 'best notion of this power'. He then quotes Richter as saying that the 'dream is an involuntary art of poetry'. Evidently, Darwin came across this phrase in Henry Maudsley's recently published *The Physiology and Pathology of the Mind*. It is not clear from Maudsley's text whether he took it from Richter's original – one of his letters – or from an intermediary source. Somewhere along the line, it seems, though, that the translation from German to English went awry. As Rycroft points out, the German word *Art* actually means 'kind', and, as a result, the phrase should probably run 'the dream is an involuntary *kind* of poetry'. It is in this form that Rycroft uses it.[1]

In the context of dream research, the link between dream and poem is golden, and for a simple reason. It offers a route around the most irritating of the obstacles that such research faces: the fact that the dream is not merely private but elusive, and, as such, provides an unsatisfactory text on which to work. The poem, in contrast, is eminently available. Like a memorandum or scientific paper, it is unequivocally *there*: a text in the public eye. When in doubt about its formal properties, one can go back to it time and again, and discuss it until misunderstandings are resolved. Where the dream may slip and slide, the dream-like properties of the poem can be unpacked at leisure, one at a time.

At first sight, this method may seem odd, especially as criticism in the arts rarely takes quite the form that the psychologist needs. Nevertheless, there are excellent precedents, not least the use of mathematical models in getting to grips with the brain and its functions. In exploiting such an analogy, there is always the risk of over-simplification, of course: a dream is not in fact a poem any more than a brain is a computer. One must be willing to contrast as well as to compare, and expect points of difference to be as revealing as points of similarity. But, with that reservation, the method contained in Richter's phrase has deep attractions, and it also has the weight of precedent on its side.

Before setting Richter's phrase to work, there is still a little steadying to do. For if the insight it conveys is in essence correct, it is in one more subtle respect misleading. So, before characterising the dream-like in literature, and giving examples, a page or two must be spent on minor adjustments.

Richter's phrase claims both dream and poem as vehicles of the imagination, dream and poem differing, it suggests, in that the dream arrives unbidden whereas the poem does not. But in fact, poems, like a great deal of waking thought, often seem involuntary too – especially in their first draft stage. The real differences between dream and poem lie elsewhere.

It is a defining characteristic of the dream that it arrives of its own accord. Unless we train ourselves specially, we exert no control over the images that follow one another onto our private cinema screens. But the solution to a crossword clue; the sudden insight that explains an evil smell in the household's drains; the sudden resolution to take a holiday or a lover; the name of an acquaintance unexpectedly re-met; the name of a familiar plant that hovers for a while just out of reach: all these can arrive in a flash, and in a sense are involuntary too. Before the flash occurs, we have often tried to remember, to work things out. We know how to wrack our brains. But the solution itself characteristically arrives in its own time. We cannot reach it down, as though it were a book from a shelf. It pops out at us more like bread from a toaster.

The same holds for our competences. When we speak or write animatedly, we no sooner place each word in its correct place than a pianist – consciously, reflectively – places each note in a cadenza. We can set ourselves to deliberate, and are perfectly capable both of meaning what we say and saying what we mean. But the pace of speech, and of our other skilled performances, is too great to permit even the semblance of conscious marshalling, assembly or control.

It is this lack of access to the processes of our own thought that has led some authorities on the brain to say that all thought is unconscious; that what we have access to is not the process of thought but only its products. Karl Lashley seems to have taken this view.[2] If Lashley was even half right, unconscious thought is a category that embraces the sleeping and waking alike. What is at issue is not the consciousness or unconsciousness of thought; rather the extent to which our thoughts, when they do arrive in consciousness, accord with some previously conceived intention or plan. We are startled when, figuratively speaking, we show ourselves the 'wrong' film. Dreams, like certain of our waking thoughts, are surprises that we spring on ourselves when off our guard.

In his excellent and unjustly neglected book, *The Psychology of Invention in the Mathematical Field*, Jacques Hadamard discusses the phenomenon of 'unconscious work': occasions when solutions to the problems, particularly of mathematics, science and music, arrive without warning. The standard format for such solutions is that of a period of intense concentration, followed by one of rest or distraction. The solution then springs out – toast-like – in a moment. There are important variants, even so, and in some at least Lashley's view of the unconsciousness of thought seems threatened. Hadamard describes mathematicians like Poincaré and Ferrol as being present, as interested spectators, at their own unconscious work. Ferrol said, for example: 'It often seems to me, especially when I am alone, that I find myself in another world. Ideas of numbers seem to live. Suddenly, questions of any kind rise before my eyes with their answers.'[3] In a number of the cases that Hadamard cites, one has the sense of a world of mathematical ideas that pursues its own purposes largely independent of the mathematician's conscious intentions: a dream-like space in which questions and answers mate of their own accord.

Often, in the world of novels and poems, it is the impulse to write for the first time that comes as a surprise. The novelist Jean Rhys speaks in her unfinished autobiography of the occasion on which this need struck her first. She describes buying quill pens from a shop – red, blue, green, yellow – on the ground that they would cheer up her room. At the same time, she noticed black exercise books on the counter, the stiff covers shiny, the spine and edges red, the pages ruled. She took several – 'I didn't know why, just because I liked the look of them.'

'It was after supper that night – as usual a glass of milk and some bread and cheese – that it happened. My fingers tingled, and the palms of my hands. I pulled a chair up to the table, opened an exercise book, and wrote *This is my Diary*. But it wasn't a diary. I remembered everything that had happened to me in the last year and a half. . . . I wrote on until late into the night, till I was so tired that I couldn't go on, and I fell into bed and slept. Next morning I remembered at once, and my only thought was to go on with the writing.'

It is tempting to assume that this sudden burst of eloquence led Jean Rhys at once into a career as a writer. It did not.

'I filled three exercise books and half another, and then I wrote: "Oh, God, I'm only twenty and I'll have to go on living and living and living." I knew then that it was finished and that there was no more to say. I put the exercise books at the bottom of my suitcase and piled my underclothes on them. After that whenever I moved I took the exercise books but I never looked at them again for many years.'[4]

Sometimes what appears so suddenly to a writer is not the possibility of writing, but a particular form of access to his subject-matter. His biographer, Painter, describes Marcel Proust, already established as an author, as reaching a point in his career when he needed, and providentially found, a prophet – John Ruskin – who would tell him that 'the artist is only a scribe'. Ruskin, through his writing, was to persuade Proust that 'the true function of the imagination is, paradoxically, not to imagine – in the sense of inventing or transforming – but to see: to see the reality which is concealed by habit and the phenomenal world.'[5]

Painter also describes in detail the celebrated moment when, for Proust, this access began. Ill as usual, Proust was persuaded by his maid to drink a cup of tea in place of his habitual coffee. Dipping a finger of dried toast into the tea and lifting the soggy mixture to his mouth he 'caught an elusive scent of geraniums and orange-blossom, mingled with the sensation of extraordinary light and happiness. Not daring to move, clinging to the taste on his palate, he pondered, until suddenly the doors of memory opened.' On the strength of what he saw through those doors, Proust was to generate a text of nearly a million and a quarter words, À la Recherche du Temps Perdu, a feat that was to take him thirteen years, and was scarcely complete when he died in 1922.

The writer's relationship to his text is often more somnambulistic than Proust's, however. In *Ways of Escape*, Graham Greene speaks of learning to trust 'the divagations of the mind': 'If you let the reins loose the horse will find its way home.' At another point, he likens himself to 'a dreamer who watches his dream unfold without power to alter its course'. In the labour of writing a novel, there are:

> 'periods of great weariness, but at any moment the unexpected might happen – a minor character would suddenly take control and dictate his words and actions. Somewhere near the beginning, for no reason I knew, I would insert an incident which seemed entirely irrelevant, and sixty thousand words later, with a sense of excitement, I would realise why it was there – the narrative had been working all that time outside my conscious control.'[6]

The evidence suggests, in other words, various forms of access on the writer's part to the experiences he wishes his sentences to convey. Ideas may reach consciousness either polished or rough-hewn. They may arrive abruptly, like a visitation, or be more continuously accessible. And they may assert themselves imperatively, or – as the film-maker Ingmar Bergman implies – they may need continual tact and coaxing.[7]

What, though, of the texts themselves – those, more specifically, that are poetic, in the sense that they cast a spell on the reader, enthralling him? In ordinary prose, there are regularities: a punctuation, both literal and metaphorical, that allows the reader to steady himself, figuratively to arrange his clothing; a framework within which implicit promises are made and kept about stages that will be set, a plot that will unfold, and, in the end, a *dénouement* that will be reached. The poetic text offers, in contrast, the appearance of freedom. Its images, ideas and narrative fragments jostle against one another and are conglomerated in surprising ways. Every variety of ambiguity threatens, and the rule of common sense is abandoned, though in a good cause.

It is only the appearance of freedom, however, that the poetic text provides. As William Gass says, the poetic sentence serves as a 'container of consciousness': an assemblage of words that presents the reader with an otherwise elusive state of mind. From the point of view of writer and reader alike, such sentences permit 'miraculous moments': pebbles turn into syllables, 'stones sound'. But underlying these transformations, there is a great deal more than a trance-like abandonment to intuition – in fact, several species of cunning.[8]

At the heart of the technical problem that the novelist or poet faces is our tendency, as readers, to distance ourselves from whatever we find in front of us. Whereas the dreamer is *in* his dream, and all sense of irony or distance is cancelled, the waking reader is anchored in the prosaic. Even if he is beguiled briefly, it is to the bedrock of common sense that he returns. The poet's task, in other words, is not to titillate his reader's imagination nor to release him on a brief flight of fancy that leaves his prosaic understanding intact. It is to destabilise that prosaic understanding, and replace it with one that is deeper.

In constructing his 'containers' the author has at his command a variety of stylistic devices: on the one hand those, such as incongruity and elision, that are in obvious but relatively superficial ways dream-like in their effect; and on the other, those which reaffirm a sense of distance, like irony and anticlimax. The poetic text is not a rag-bag of tricks, though. When successful, it is an edifice with a strong if implicit sense of design. Characteristically, this design is one in which antithetical forces are at work, and there exist tensions that cannot be resolved. It is on these tensions – unresolvable but contained – that the more profoundly dream-like properties of a text usually prove in the end to depend.

It is the aim of this chapter and the next to dwell on this question of design; to show how tensions can be created within a text and, once created, contained. Two examples are used. The first is a scene from a recent novel. This successfully establishes an atmosphere of waking hallucination, almost nightmare, yet does so by conspicuously undramatic means. The second, altogether more tightly knit, is a poem, and here the effects are achieved more parsimoniously, by exploiting ambiguities that are more narrowly semantic and concern the multiplicity of meanings that attach to certain words.

Far from fostering in his reader the need to enter greedily into certain imagined scenes like a voyeur, the novelist who aims to create a dream-like state does so by subjecting him to a dislocating series of pushes and tugs. The tension that results can echo that of the real dream with remarkable precision, as a passage from J. G. Farrell's novel *The Siege of Krishnapur* demonstrates. This chronicles an episode in the Indian Mutiny. It is a book with the conventional narrative structure of a historical adventure, and it exerts a powerful grip. Its impact is oddly spectral, nonetheless, even at times surreal.

At the centre of *The Siege of Krishnapur*, there is a set-piece. Although the siege of a small outpost of Empire has begun in earnest, famine and disease have yet to bite home, and the social proprieties of the English in India are still being preserved. The chief actors are Fleury, the young thinker, and his friend Harry, the soldier. It is a scene that centres on Lucy Hughes: spoilt, self-concerned, and ostracised by all the other white women because she had an affair – all, that is, except Harry's beautiful sister, Louise. Despite her ostracism, Lucy is the focus of certain domestic niceties. She has her favourites, and gives them tea parties among the smashed remnants of the banqueting hall's furniture. Fleury and Harry protect her, and are attending one of these parties as the set-piece begins.[9]

It is the rainy season, and with the rain come dense clouds of cockchafers: 'black as pitch and quite harmless, but with a sickening odour which they lent to anything they touched'. As the kettle boils for the second round of tea, a cloud of cockchafers billows through the window and envelops the entire party. The bugs show a special preference for Lucy: 'Poor Lucy! Her nerves had already been in a bad enough state. She leapt to her feet with a cry which was instantly stifled by a mouthful of insects. She beat at her face, her bosom, her stomach, her hips, with hands which looked as if they were dripping with damson jam.' She rips off her clothes ('this was no time to worry about modesty'), and 'there she stood, stark naked but as black and glistening as an African slave-girl. How those flying bugs loved Lucy's white skin! Hardly had her damson-dripping fingers scooped a long white furrow from her thigh to her breast before the blackness would swirl back over it.'

The stuff of nightmares! Abandoning the attempt to clean herself, she stands motionless with horror. Fleury and Harry exchange a glance of 'shock and bewilderment at the unfortunate turn the tea party had suddenly taken'. The while, an effervescent mass of bugs detaches itself from one of Lucy's breasts, 'revealed to be the shape of a plump carp, then from one of her diamond knee-caps, then an ebony avalanche thundered from her spine down over her buttocks, then from some other part of her.'

The scene is dream-like in content rather than in style. In fact, Farrell's style seems to slip continually towards that of *Girl's Own* magazine, the ineffably polite. And having created this dissonance between dream-like subject-matter and prosaic style, odd in itself, Farrell then executes a step from narrative into philosophy, creating as he does so a dislocation of an even stranger kind:

'But hardly had a white part been exposed before blackness covered it again. This coming and going of black and white was just fast enough to give a faint, flickering image of Lucy's delightful nakedness and all of a sudden gave Fleury an idea. Could one have a series of daguerreotypes which would give the impression of movement? "I must invent the 'moving daguerreotype' later on when I have a moment to spare", he told himself, but an instant later this important idea had gone out of his mind, for this was an emergency.'

Lucy faints, still covered with black bugs. Fleury and Harry then set about scraping her naked body clean, using the covers of a Bible for the purpose, 'sacred boards', that they use 'as if they were giant razor blades'. Together, they 'shave the black foam of insects off Lucy's skin'. In the course of this operation, they discover – as Ruskin is said to have discovered of his own wife on their wedding night – that Lucy has pubic hair.

'This caused them a bit of a surprise at first. It was not something that had ever occurred to them as possible, likely, or even desirable. "D'you think this is *supposed* to be here?" asked Harry, who had spent a moment or two scraping at it ineffectually with his board. Because the hair, too, was black, it was hard to be sure that it was not simply matted and dried insects. "That's odd", said Fleury, peering at it with interest; he had never seen anything like it on a statue. "Better leave it, anyway, for the time being. We can always come back to it later when we have done the rest".'

After these events, and after everything that Farrell seeks to say through them about young men like Fleury and Harry and their relation to the opposite sex – and says, advertently or inadvertently, about attitudes of his own – the siege continues. The defenders' degradation increases beyond measure. In the end, relief comes, but by then they are shrunken with starvation and stinking: Lucy's breasts are no longer like plump carp, 'more like plaice or Dover sole'. In his last pages, Farrell goes out of his way to ensure that normality is reaffirmed. Harry becomes a general in due course; Lucy marries him and becomes a general's wife. Fleury marries Harry's sister Louise, goes back to London and becomes a patron of the arts:

'It is surprising how quickly the survivors returned to the civilised life they had been living before. Only sometimes in dreams the terrible days of the siege, which were like the dark foundation of the civilised life they had returned to, would return years later to visit them: they would awake, terrified and sweating, to find themselves in white starched linen, in a comfortable bed, in peaceful England. And all would be well.'

Or would it? Are we reassured, either on our own behalf or on those of his characters? Only, I think, in the sense that one is reassured, having awoken, that a nightmare is over. We know that something closely analogous can happen again. It is Farrell's gift to hold us in suspense, neither able to abandon ourselves to the world of nightmare, as in a horror film, nor to find security elsewhere.

Admired for the surreal nature of his effects, Farrell's dislocations are nonetheless subtle. Rarely do they announce themselves as did those of the surreal film-makers, painters and poets of the 1920s and 1930s. The dislocation is insidiously successful precisely because it is not advertised. As the surrealists advocated, Farrell makes great use of dreams in his novels, but instead of using them to destabilise and subvert common sense, he employs them in the routine work of establishing character and advancing plot. Here and there, dreams even help him create small islands of reassurance.

In another novel, *The Singapore Grip*, in which Farrell chronicles the collapse of the British colony in the face of invading Japanese during the Second World War, he devotes a whole chapter to the dreams of the colony's inhabitants, slumbering while the Japanese bombers head towards them, starlight glinting on silver wings, 'slipping through the clear skies like fish through a sluice-gate'. A grossly dissolute and unprincipled young man, Monty Blackett, is one of the slumberers. Instead of the anxieties or debauches that one might expect, his dreams are filled with those images of 'purity and love without limit' that Farrell suggests we may each carry with us, buried beneath 'the dross of tainted circumstances and the limits of living from one day to the next', and that can ring through our sleeping thoughts 'like the chime of a bell on a frosty morning'.[10]

The moral is simple, if not entirely obvious. One creates dream-like scenes not by describing the phenomena in question, nor even by using in isolation those stylistic devices, elision for example, that are obviously dream-like. One does it by establishing equivalents: groupings of ideas that re-create, within the waking sphere, the formal properties of sleeping thought. The dream-like text is one that maintains a state of tension: in this case, between the forces of the narrative convention and those of unforeseen and unpredictable dislocation – the very mirror of our night life, our own dreams.[11]

Notes

(1) Darwin (1871), p. 45 and (1887), p. 74; Rycroft (1979), p. 40. Richter's phrase occurs on p. 193 of Maudsley's (1868) text, Darwin's reference to it seeming to be inaccurate. Just

conceivably, 'art' is a misprint for 'part'. In the absence of the German original, we have no means of telling.

(2) Lashley (1958). At first glance, Lashley's view seems to rule out the use of introspection in psychology. In practice, it remains vital. It helps us write the brain's 'specification': that list of performance characteristics that any model of the brain must explain if it is to be taken seriously. Without it, one might as well seek to explain the orbit of Mars without first looking through a telescope.

(3) Hadamard (1945), p. 59; see also his comments on Mozart.

(4) Rhys (1981), p. 128. Her first book was not to appear for a further seven years, and the autobiographical scenes set out in her exercise books not for a further fourteen, when they were published reworked, as *Voyage in the Dark*.

(5) Painter (1983), pp. 240 and 448. Proust's impassioned interest in Ruskin was in some ways reminiscent of Ruskin's no less passionate devotion to the paintings of Turner. Despite only the sketchiest command of English, Proust devoted several years of his life to translating Ruskin's books into French.

(6) Greene (1981), pp. 208 and 220. Both Rycroft (1979) and McKellar (1979) discuss the altogether more extreme experience of Enid Blyton. Her books were shown to her, it seems, on 'a private cinema screen'. She describes them as coming from her 'under-mind'. 'To write book after book without knowing what is to be said or done sounds silly, and yet it happens. Sometimes a character makes a joke, a really funny one that makes me laugh as I type it on my paper – and I think "Well, I couldn't have thought of that myself in a hundred years!" And then I think, "Well, *who* did think of it then?" '

(7) Bergman has likened inspiration to 'a brightly coloured thread sticking out of the dark sack of the unconscious'. If he winds this thread up, and does it with care, he says, a complete film results: quoted by Kinder (1980), p. 62.

(8) Gass (1976).

(9) Farrell (1975), pp. 252 and 343.

(10) Farrell (1978), p. 125.

(11) The same holds, Gass claims, for the art of making sentences

'blue' or sexual. One does this not by using sexual words, or describing sexual activities, but by exploiting the language's formal and metaphoric powers. Evidence bearing on the tension between the story-telling and more disruptive components of dream thought is described in Chapter 10.

CHAPTER SEVEN

The Involuntary and
the Ambiguous

I would now like to consider in more detail the question of ambiguity. In a text like Farrell's *The Siege of Krishnapur*, the ambiguities are typically those of stance and style rather than of the meanings of particular words or phrases. It is in poetry that ambiguities in the language itself become a prime concern; and it is here that poems and dreams can at times seem so alike as to be subsumable within the same interpretative frame.

The moment has come to examine the extent to which the poet's use of ambiguity can be systematic, serving not just to create a suitably evocative atmosphere, but to fashion webs or networks of associative meaning within which elusive aspects of experience can successfully be contained and, once contained, conveyed. The example chosen is that of the German poet Rainer Maria Rilke. He has already been belaboured elsewhere, but his experience is too apposite to omit.[1] Both in terms of its involuntary nature, and in terms of the inherent ambiguity of the works he wrote, it neatly captures much of what must be said about the intimate parallels between poem and dream. More than that, it prefigures the second principle on which the present argument rests: the relation of the dream (or, in this case, the poem) to its waking context.

When he sat down to write on a memorable day in February 1922, Rilke, then a man in his mid-forties, was expecting to finish a long-delayed task: that of writing the *Duino Elegies*. But what happened was as involuntary as any dream. For what he in fact wrote were the first twenty-six *Sonnets to Orpheus*. A year later, he wrote of the *Sonnets* to a friend:

'Now and then they may show some lack of consideration for the reader. Even to me, in their rising up and imposing themselves upon me, they are perhaps the most mysterious, most enigmatic, dictation I have ever endured and performed;

the whole first part was written down in a single breathless obedience, between the 2nd and 5th of February 1922, without one word's being in doubt or requiring to be altered. And that at a time when I had got myself ready for another large work and was already busy with it.'[2]

The suggestion here is that Rilke had no prior warning of the *Sonnets* whatsoever. That is not quite so. There were two precipitating events. At the beginning of January, a friend, Frau Gertrud Ouckama Knoop, had sent him the journal she had kept during the fatal illness of her daughter Wera, who had died in her late teens. Rilke had only seen Wera once or twice when she was still a child. In a letter written after the *Sonnets* had been completed, he describes her in the following terms:

'This lovely child who began with dancing and excited wonder in all who then saw her through her body's and mind's inborn art of motion and transformation, unexpectedly declared to her mother that she neither could nor would dance any longer . . . her body strangely altered, became, without losing its beautiful eastern contours, strangely heavy and massive . . . (which was already the beginning of that mysterious glandular disease which was so quickly to bring on death). . . . During the time that still remained for her Wera pursued music, finally she did nothing but sketch – as though the dancing which had been denied were, more and more gently, more and more discreetly, still issuing from her.'

The second precipitating event was simpler than the first. One day, he saw in a shop window a small engraving of Orpheus with his lyre. He claimed afterwards, that 'in a flash, the *Sonnets* had grouped themselves around this figure and given themselves its name'. He also said that the *Sonnets* had lightly attached themselves to the vanished figure of Wera Knoop, and that he perceived this connection more and more as he wrote, eventually dedicating them to her as 'a monument'.

Looking back over the preceding years, we see an established poet lapsing for a period of a decade into depression, his work coming only in dribs and drabs. In modern parlance, Rilke was 'blocked'. As a young man, he had written 'incessantly, both in prose and verse' and was 'full of ambitious projects for the foundation of literary journals and the production of plays'.[3] But throughout the war years, he produced little – even, for months on end, nothing.

An event, Wera Knoop's death, stirs in him certain abiding themes: those of love and death. It is understandable that it should do so, an extant photograph showing Wera to have possessed an exceptional, and disturbingly adult, beauty.[4] These themes attach themselves in an instant to an appropriate but by no means especially remarkable image: that of Orpheus and his lyre. Abruptly, the poet begins to write with great fluency, as if taking dictation, and, as he writes, he detects increasingly the connection between his *Sonnets* and what might be called the initial stimulus, Wera Knoop herself. Only two of the *Sonnets* are addressed directly to Wera – the last but one in the first series, the last but one in the second – but they are dedicated to her and revolve around her. There is the clear impression, in other words, that, in each series of *Sonnets*, the first of twenty-six poems, the second of twenty-nine, he is working his way round to addressing Wera directly; and that, having done so, his drive to express himself in this particular mode is satisfied, in the first instance temporarily, in the second more permanently.[5]

As a symbol, Orpheus was well suited to Rilke's need. His musical eloquence left wild beasts spellbound, and love for his wife Eurydice led him to enter Hades to plead for her life. Also attractive to Rilke must have been Orpheus' other-worldliness and commitment to the notion of purity. Heir to the more carnal Dionysians, who encouraged a violent oscillation between states of drunken orgy and ones of spirituality, Orpheus was seen as embodying calmer and more passive virtues – a mediator who opened the secrets of the natural world by means of his art. There could in addition have been an element of masochistic attraction for Rilke in Orpheus' fate. Having lost Eurydice in a careless glance, he retreated from the world, and was torn to pieces for his pains by the envious hands of the Thracian women.

Orpheus is thus the idealised personification of all those men who are devotedly heterosexual, indeed passionately so, but who are themselves somewhat androgynous. Rather than being, in the psychoanalytic jargon, 'phallic' males, at liberty to impose their wills and needs on the world around them, they are at heart passive, and open as a result not only to the rapacities of others, but also, one suspects, to the involuntary. Orpheus was thus an object of identification for Rilke. As he had once written to Lou Andreas-Salomé, for a while his mistress,

'I am like the little anemone I once saw in the garden at Rome; throughout the day it had opened so wide that it could no longer shut at the approach of night! It was frightful to see it on the dark meadow, wide open, still absorbing into its almost madly flung open calyx, and above it the far too large night that was not yet done.'

It must, though, have been Orpheus' access to the worlds of the living and the dead that enabled Rilke to move, vicariously, from the pain and waste of Wera Knoop's death to a conception of human experience that encompasses life and death as complementary elements. 'Two innermost experiences were decisive,' he says, for the production of the *Sonnets* and the *Elegies*: first, the 'deeply growing resolve to keep life open towards death'; and, second, the 'intellectual necessity of instating the transformations of love' within a frame of reference that includes death rather than denying it.

Plainly, Rilke's experiences as a 'receiver' place him out of the ordinary run. We all, from time to time, experience the constellation of thought around an evocative symbol: in his case, a print of Orpheus and lyre, in ours a song, perhaps, or an old photograph. It is primarily the quantity and precision of the sentences that flowed through his mind and onto the page that set him apart.

In less than three weeks, Rilke produced well over a thousand lines of pithy compacted poetry. The *Sonnets* and *Elegies* thus offer a vast abundance of texts to work on. The one chosen, not for the first time, is perhaps the most familiar of the sonnets, the one about the unicorn. In Leishman's translation, it runs:

This is the creature there has never been.
They never knew it, and yet, none the less,
they loved the way it moved, its suppleness,
its neck, its very gaze, mild and serene.

Not there, because they loved it, it behaved
as though it were. They always left some space.
And in that clear unpeopled space they saved
it lightly reared its head, with scarce a trace

of not being there. They fed it, not with corn,
but only with the possibility
of being. And that was able to confer

such strength, its brow put forth a horn. One horn.
Whitely it stole up to a maid, – to *be*
within the silver mirror and in her.

This sonnet creates a strong impression of ambiguity: not just of words and phrases that are ambiguous in isolation, but of relationships between words and phrases that are ambiguous and that resonate on one another in ways that are likewise ambiguous. It is a troublesome legacy of Anglo-Saxon philosophy that such ambiguities are equated either with pretentiousness or with muddle; with froth or rubbish. Such prejudices exist to be violated, of course; and violate we must if we are to make sense of the poet's craft. In the hands of the sufficiently skilled, ambiguity is a property of words that gives us access to just those recesses of experience that other modes of expression fail to reach. And if the task of teasing out the ambiguities from a given text seems wearisome, its justification, in the present context, is that it yields a framework within which to set the dream.

How does one proceed? There is no harm in being empirical. Just as we wake people in sleep laboratories and ask them to report their dreams, so we can invite them to read Rilke's sonnet and to report those of its ideas that linger most vividly in the mind. A virtue of this method is that it admits, at once, that individuals' readings may differ: that there is no correct reading that we expect all readers to home in on, but a variety of readings which, with time and patience, we may be able to reconcile. The movement towards a 'best reading' is not a matter of consensus, still less of calculating averages and standard deviations. It is a matter of argument that centres on what the text 'says'.

For the sake of the example, assume that the first person we invite to read the sonnet reports three ideas as especially vivid:

The unicorn itself
The silver mirror
The phrase 'Whitely it stole up to a maid'

There already exist techniques in psychology which, when suitably adapted, could help us execute the next step: the establishment of clusters of associations for each of the three remembered elements. In response to the first element, the unicorn, our reader might produce these four clusters:

(i) White, purity, serenity, moonlight . . .
(ii) Horn, rhinoceros, aphrodisiacs . . .
(iii) Heraldry (the lion and unicorn), tapestries, coats of arms . . .
(iv) Corn, horses, the smells of stabling, zoos, dung . . .

It requires no great feat of intuition to see that these clusters presuppose at least two dimensions of meaning. Also that the position of the unicorn on each dimension is equivocal. Initially, Rilke creates a somewhat ethereal setting for his creature, but by the time the last line is reached, it is 'within' both the silver mirror and the maid, and altogether earthier possibilities can legitimately be envisaged. One dimension contrasts purity and moonlight on the one hand, horns, dung and aphrodisiacs on the other: the Platonic with the Carnal. The second dimension contrasts Real with Imaginary: rhinoceroses in their cages and horses in their stables, as opposed to the mythical lion and unicorn of tapestry and coat of arms. As far as this particular reader is concerned, then, there are four unicorns, not one:

Unicorn-as-Platonic-Love
Unicorn-as-Carnal-Lust
Unicorn-as-Mammal
Unicorn-as-Mythical-Beast

There may be other unicorns. The point of the example is that there are four at least. We try to reconcile Unicorn-as-Platonic-Love with Unicorn-as-Carnal-Lust, Unicorn-as-Mammal with Unicorn-as-Mythical-Beast, and a sense of tension results. Within a factual memorandum such tensions should not arise. Where they do, they can usually be resolved. But in the space created by Rilke's sonnet, they not only exist but multiply, creating resonances and dissonances that are only partly within either poet's or reader's control. They may push the reader, what is more, towards personal discoveries that he might not otherwise make. In the present instance, they may enable him to recognise that, in certain episodes of his own intimate life, the Carnal and the Platonic have coexisted in baffling and apparently irreconcilable ways. It is presumably no accident that the 'space' created in a poem like Rilke's, in which relationships are ambiguous and movement closely constrained but not frozen, should so closely resemble not only that of certain sorts of dream, but also that of sexual fantasies: those curiously ritualised scenes that enact themselves in some minds' eyes during sexual intercourse.[6]

The knowledge and sensibility that a reader brings to bear on such a text is of significance, just as it is in reporting a dream. He may be only dimly aware of unicorns in tapestries and on coats of arms. Alternatively, he may have a scholarly knowledge of the ancient bestiaries, and of the myths of the 'virgin capture' and the 'holy hunt'.[7] He may be knowledgeable about the anthropological literature on aphrodisiacs and the trade in rhinoceros horns, narwhal tusks. All this will prime him to respond to Rilke's words in one way as opposed to others. Finally, though, it is the words themselves that create the setting within which his efforts to make sense are cast; and, to that extent, it is the text that is sovereign.

The second element in this particular reader's recollection – the silver mirror – is no less ambiguous than the first. Here, too, the uncertainties are of an obviously conceptual nature. The first concerns the role of the mirror either as a reflective surface, as in physics, or as a porthole on the realm of the imaginary, as in *Alice*:

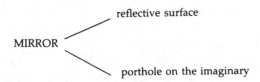

But a moment's thought shows that each of these readings is unstable. A reflective surface can serve either as an instrument of cold-eyed self-appraisal or as an adjunct to the task of making-up, of self-beautification. The porthole, similarly, may open onto a world of surreal fantasy, the land of the melted watch and fur-lined teacup, or onto one in which musings are more narcissistic and personal. Each of the initial readings sub-divides, in other words:

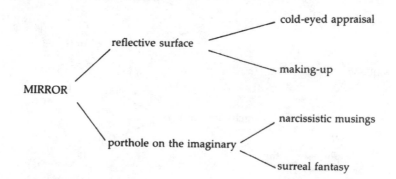

There are now four readings, not one. Even so, they are not entirely at odds with one another; there is the sense among them of a limited degree of convergence, as though a centrally placed interpretative theme might yet emerge. The notion of beautifying oneself is, after all, not a million miles distant from that of Narcissus beside his dewy pool.

Although the pattern of interpretative reasoning is already complex, there is more to follow. Making-up can be a feat of dissimulation; a question of 'putting on a face', as impersonal as putting on a bandage. Or it can allow the discovery of the self as an eroticised object: something that can gleam and glitter in the beholder's eye. Likewise, on the tree's lower branch, Narcissus beside his pool can imply, as in the legend, a passive pining; alternatively, it can suggest a more positive vision or fantasy around which a way of life can be constructed and in which a sense of beauty is the driving force. The tree has branched again. There are now six readings (or twigs), not four.

Is any one of these readings, or any grouping of them, the 'correct' one – or is there a natural democracy among interpretations of ambiguous signs that prevents any achieving supremacy? The answer, plainly, is that it is part of the poet's skill, like the gardener's, to direct our attention along certain paths; to bias our perception of the spaces he creates so that we will tend to favour certain avenues at the expense of others.

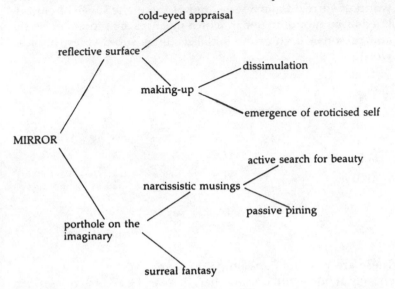

In the prose of the memorandum, the writer can erect signposts: 'To the Arboretum', 'Teas', 'Exit'. The poet plays for higher stakes and takes greater risks. At one level, he relies on nudges and hints to control the direction his reader takes: reverberations and echoes of meaning, scraps of narrative and the rhythm of his words. At another level, as we shall see in a moment, he can also draw upon the implicit strength of his design.

In a novel, narrative and design or structure are easily confused; it is tempting (though mistaken) to see the design of a book like *The Siege of Krishnapur* in terms of its plot. In poetry, the distinction is all-important. Rilke's sonnet about the unicorn is one in which little happens, and what does happen is ambiguous. 'Whitely it stole up to a maid . . .', the third of our reader's recollections, is the phrase that plays a vital part in this narrative. Grammatically, it is ordinary enough: it has subject, verb and object. In isolation, there is little doubt what it means. It stands, on the other hand, between two more phrases, and when all three are taken in sequence, their ambiguity is unavoidable. In the line before, the creature has 'put forth a horn'. In the line after, it is 'within the silver mirror and in her'. It might be stealing up on the maiden timidly; it might be contemplating rape.

The question of design is another matter altogether. It is plainly Rilke's intention to hold his readers not within a single ambiguity, but among several. In their turn, these ambiguities cut quite deeply into our assumptions about the nature of desire. They also appear to converge. Rather than being scattered in a variety of unrelated directions, they seem in some way to interlock. In order to make the nature of this interlocking explicit, one must go back to basics, and consider thought in terms not of its nuances but of distinctions that are altogether more element-ary. From these simple distinctions, formats of surprising subtlety can quite quickly be derived.

In the simplest terms of all, one can characterise thought as being either closed or open-ended, as either convergent or divergent.[8] The closed, convergent or problem-solving mode is often exemplified in riddles:

Question: 'What is it that is pink all over, white all over, weighs sixty pounds and frightens the neighbours?'

Here, four categories of objects are offered, and appear un-related, even mutually exclusive. The solution lies in the discovery or invention of a fifth category to which all four will be seen to belong: in this case, that fifth category is 'bull terrier'. It is satisfactory in as much as it leaves no loose ends, or, if it does, that it is tidier than its rivals. It is a mode, obviously, that embraces a great deal besides the riddle: many sorts of detective work, most items in IQ tests, all those issues in science where apparently disparate bodies of evidence can convincingly be reconciled – any thought, in fact, where problems can be posed and a uniquely satisfactory solution sought.

Formally, the relation of the four categories – (a) pink all over, (b) white all over, (c) weighs sixty pounds, and (d) frightens the neighbours – to the fifth category, (e) bull terrier, can be summarised in this familiar diagram:

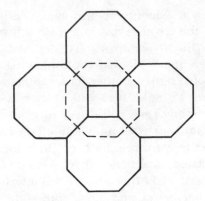

This pattern appeared in Chapter 4, where it had a different but analogous task to perform: that of summarising the relationship of rival dream interpretations both to one another and to the dream. The point of such diagrams is precisely their generality. They can be used to formalise all manner of relationships between ideas: those in interpretative work, where it is its central 'cell' – whether dream or poem – that is given, and the additional cells that are constructed around it, or those in science, problem-solving or riddles, where it is the peripheral cells, the elements of the problem, that are given, and it is the central one that has to be discovered or created.

Once complete, interpretative reasoning and science are more alike than they seem. But what these cell diagrams fail to reveal, and what is of particular importance here, is the direction of the argument while it is still unfolding; its movement from what is given towards what must be constructed. So, in place of cell patterns, one needs arrows.[9] The riddle of the bull terrier, then, looks like this:

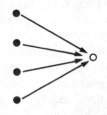

By no means all problems are solved neatly, in a single step; nor are their elements always simple. Frequently the solution is reached by means of successive approximations; an argument or dialectic in which each step constitutes a claim or story, in which several propositions are linked. As the argument unfolds, each new version is confronted by objections and counter-claims, and the elements of the story as a result evolve, both in themselves and in relation to one another. An example is discussed in the next chapter: Kuper and Stone's ingenious reinterpretation of Freud's dream about Irma's injection. This dream is depicted by Kuper and Stone, persuasively, not as a static scene, but as one which shuffles forward step by step, towards a 'solution':

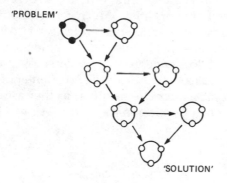

Much more is afoot inside both poems and dreams, though, than the resolution of problems, irrespective of how generously this notion is conceived. Much of their activity is open-ended, divergent:

Question: 'What is a unicorn?'
Answers: 'A mythic beast, a heraldic device, a symbol of purity . . .' and so on.

Such a pattern of reasoning is often seen as incompatible with coherence of structure, even as an attack on structure, and as an affirmation of Dionysian energy in the face of Apollonian order. This is a travesty, however, and grossly underestimates the complexity of internal organisation that poems and dreams permit. The essence of open-ended thought is that it moves from a point of departure in a variety of apparently unrelated directions. This form of thought is often characterised in terms of those reveries, free associations and fantasies in which there is no regulative intention, and no attempt is made to follow a train or sequence through to a conclusion. In practice, it contributes to the solution of tightly knit problems, in that it provides the raw material for what Einstein and others have referred to as associative or combinatory play. Much more important in the present context, the closed and open-ended can also join forces to create a third format – the 'hybrid' – that is indispensable to the understanding of 'containers of consciousness', dreams and poems alike. In this format, the closed and open-ended combine, not with one as subservient to the other, as they are in problem-solving, but as equal partners in the same design:

Question: 'What do mirrors and rock pools have in common?'
Answer: 'Both reflect.'

Some of the attributes of mirror and rock pool are shared; not just their reflective properties but their colour, for instance. But most are not shared. We read them in terms of their shared attributes if these strike us in a particular context as telling or illuminative, and allow other connotations to go their own ways. In that lies the essence of metaphor, the intuitive perception of the similarity in dissimilars.[10] In a novel or film, the resulting array, a semantic

88

landscape, may sprawl. In poems, paintings and some dreams, the design of this array is often, in comparison, compact.

Even in those arrays where the surface activity is entirely divergent, there may nevertheless be a powerful sense of design. Beyond those initial steps, there may lie a central point on which all trains of thought converge, and from which the semantic activity in the array as a whole can be surveyed:

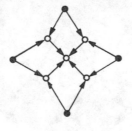

Such a scheme, to outward appearance wholly open-ended but in fact tightly coherent, can have more than one focal centre. At heart, its meaning can rest on the relation between two centrally placed propositions, not on one:

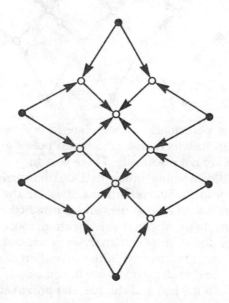

In such a pattern, there is no path that leads from one point of central focus to the other. The meaning of the array as a whole is in other words inherently ambiguous but at the same time tightly knit.

Especially with an increase in scale, it is easy to envisage arrays in which the heartland remains open, and a reading, initially a matter of analysis, becomes in the end one of empathy and intuition:

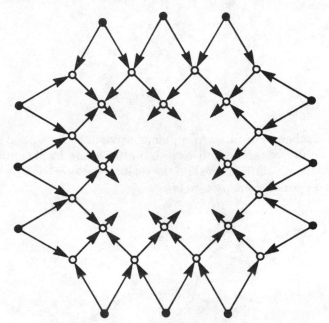

This format is particularly appropriate to bodies of ideas, like Rilke's sonnet, in which ambiguities are posed and allowed to interlock, but are not resolvable. There is in such cases no simple story to be told; nothing much that can be carried away in a nutshell. A complete interpretation consists in the identification of the text's pertinent ambiguities and contradictions, in plotting out their connections, and in the delineation, too, of the centrally placed area of doubt, in which analysis peters out and empathy takes over. It does not consist in the invention of solutions that are not there, least of all by reference to some body of theory that lies outside both the text and the life that provoked it. As Yeats, one of Rilke's approximate contemporaries, once remarked: 'We make out of the quarrel with others, rhetoric, but of the quarrel with ourselves, poetry.'[11] It is the function of the sorts of sentences that Rilke and Yeats wrote to make the terms of our quarrels with ourselves apparent, not to imply that such quarrels can be resolved.

In the event, this format embraces much more than works of art and dreams, and is one for which far-reaching claims can be made. All those ambitions we refer to colloquially as 'dreams' – whether political, like Martin Luther King's, or personal, like the fantasy of a home in a rural landscape without obnoxious neighbours or smells – are schemes with important practical implications that have at their heart a commitment that can only be grasped empathetically. It could also be said that all personal knowledge, the stuff of our relationships with those who intimately concern us, takes this form too: on the surface, questions open to painstaking analysis, evidence that can be construed with more or less intelligence or candour, but, nearer the centre, areas in which intuition is the only guide, and in which ambiguities must be left in principle unresolved.

There are wider implications even than these. For this format belongs to a larger family, all of which have in common a carefully articulated peripheral structure and a 'heartland' that is either qualitatively dissimilar from the periphery or is, in effect, empty. The discipline of psychology is a case in point.[12] Around its edges – the shaded areas in the diagram below – where the concerns of the psychologist overlap those of academic neighbours like the brain physiologist, the computer scientist and the sociologist, there are tightly elaborated bodies of research and real excitement. Towards the centre, in comparison, one finds areas of imprecision, filled with personal loyalties and emotional commitments, and with big theories about human nature, as ideological as they are vague:[13]

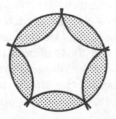

In discussing the dream, Rycroft speaks of it as 'a form of communicating or communing with oneself', and sees it as 'analogous to such waking activities as talking to oneself, reminding oneself, exhorting oneself, consoling oneself, frightening oneself, entertaining oneself or exciting oneself with one's own imagination – and, perhaps more particularly, to such waking meditative imaginative activities as summoning up remembrance of things past or envisaging the prospect of things future.'[14] If he is right, the principle embodied in Richter's phrase enables us to see how these internal communications, from ourselves to ourselves, can best be construed. We read them as poems: in first draft, perhaps, or scattered in fragments here and there, but poems all the same.

In grappling with them, we bear the stock-in-trade of the poet in mind. His special skill lies in those manoeuvres with words that create unresolved and inexplicit tensions, the most obvious and accessible of which is his exploitation of ambiguity. He uses this, not as a decorative flourish, but as a trustworthy device, helpful to him in his self-appointed task of fashioning 'containers'. And although it seems to threaten good order and strong design, in the hands of the sufficiently practised it can become integral to both.

Sometimes the design will yield a central point of vantage, from which the semantic activity in the array as a whole can be reviewed. There is no guarantee, in any one instance, whether poem or dream, that this will happen, but it perfectly well might. More often, in the case of a dream if not of a poem, there could prove to be several points of vantage, not one. A dream like Jung's about the two skulls, for instance: arguably at least, this had not one focus, but three foci that were quite distinct. It was about his desire to kill his parents, *and* about the organisation of the mind on the principle of the archaeological dig, *and* about Freud's domestic triangle in the apartment at 19 Berggasse. On other occasions still, the interpreter may well have to settle for a summary of the dream's elements, each considered separately, not through any failure of skill or stamina on his own part, but because the links between those elements are not there.[15]

In poems and dreams alike, the text guides thought, but does not regulate it. In grasping the shape of the garden which an author (or dreamer) creates, we open ourselves not only to the paths and vistas that exist in his head, but also to those that exist in our own. As John Broadbent has put it, 'we need to permit the unconscious to proffer its readings; to let ourselves dream the poem, or become a part of it.'[16] As a result of the discoveries we make about our own unexplored meanings, we may be able to respond in kind: to generate not pages of analysis, but poems (or dreams) of our own. A poem, like a dream, is a body of ideas that can release not only the 'unwritten interior texts' previously lodged in the poet's head, but those lodged in each of his readers' heads likewise.

Notes

(1) For example, in my earlier book, *The Cult of the Fact* (Hudson, 1972).

(2) Leishman (1949), pp. 9, 12 and 164.

(3) Leishman (1964), p. 10.

(4) Hudson (1975), pl. 3. Like Ruskin, Rilke may have had an erotic interest in small girls that he held guiltily in check. His relations with more mature women like Lou Andreas-Salomé were troubled – scarcely surprising in the light of the bizarre upbringing he had received. Until he was five, he was brought up as a girl. When he was nine his parents separated, and thereafter he spent five years in a state military academy, which he loathed.

(5) Some twenty years earlier, Rilke had experienced another episode of continuous inspiration. This yielded part of a cycle of sixty-seven short verse-meditations, supposed to be those of a Russian monk.

(6) Stoller's remarkable book *Sexual Excitement* (1979) is important in this context. Revealingly, Stoller likens art to sexual excitement and sees both as a search for 'controlled, managed ambiguity': Stoller (1976), p. 117.

(7) He may even have read Odell Shepard's memorable *The Lore of the Unicorn* (1930). The unicorn's history, as Shepard reveals, is tortuous. In the 'virgin capture' version of the myth, the virgin is used as bait: 'He approaches, throwing himself upon her. Then the girl offers him her breasts, and the animal begins to suck the breasts of the maiden and

conducts himself familiarly with her. Then the girl, while sitting quietly, reaches forth her hand and grasps the horn on the animal's brow, and at this point the huntsmen come up and take the beast and go away with him to the king.' The 'holy hunt' version is more predatory. The virgin lures the beast towards her by the odour of her sanctity. It is then killed by huntsmen lying in wait, and its blood used to heal the king's ailing son. By the time of the Cluny tapestries, which Rilke admired, the unicorn had lost its original strength and erotic vigour, and had become moonstruck, an effect, it seems, of the unicorn's symbolic identification with Christ, and the maiden's with the Virgin Mary.

(8) This distinction corresponds only very roughly to Freud's between the secondary and primary and to Susanne Langer's between the discursive and non-discursive: see Rycroft (1979), p. 13.

(9) Technically, these diagrams are called digraphs. Their formal properties are discussed by Foulkes (1978), pp. 302–21. The use made of them here, though, differs in character from his.

(10) Modern linguists and linguistic philosophers pay little attention to the role of metaphor in ordinary language. As if by some tacit agreement to avoid the ambiguous, the indeterminate or the 'fuzzy', metaphor has been treated as 'a device of the poetic imagination and the rhetorical flourish – a matter of extraordinary rather than ordinary language'. Lakoff and Johnson's recent book, *Metaphors We Live By*, is an antidote to this prejudice, and a text, too, immediately accessible to the psychologist. Its claim is 'that metaphor is pervasive in everyday life, not just in language but in thought and action. Our ordinary conceptual system, in terms of which we both think and act, is fundamentally metaphorical in nature': Lakoff and Johnson (1980), p. 3.

(11) Quoted by Leishman (1964), p. 22.

(12) It is sometimes argued that all human knowledge, whether within science or outside it, is inseparable from human interest: see, for example, Habermas (1972). The tendency of such critiques is to foster a deep scepticism about the existence of knowledge that is in any important sense objective. More to the point, perhaps, is the realisation that

all disciplines conform, to a greater or less extent, to the pattern adumbrated here: a carefully structured surface of 'hard' knowledge and analytical technique, but, nearer the centre, commitments that are fervent yet imprecise. While everyone in academic life can identify a chemist, few seem able to articulate at all plainly the theoretical principles that separate chemistry as a discipline from, say, physics.

(13) Hudson, in press.

(14) Rycroft (1979), p. 45.

(15) Structuralists like Kuper and Stone (1982) assume that all dreams have a coherent internal architecture, and that they move from 'problem' to 'solution'. Here, such a pattern is treated as one among many. Some are less internally coherent; some equally so, but designed along different lines.

(16) Broadbent (1982). The network of relationships linking artist, text and audience is discussed in the context of the visual arts in Hudson (1982), pp. 138–50. It is a network peppered with paradox and surprise.

CHAPTER EIGHT

The Waking Context

The position of the dream interpreter is in significant respects weak when compared with that of someone making sense of a poem. Not only is the dream elusive, it may lack internal structure to a degree that in a finished poem is rare. On the other hand, the dream interpreter can often discover a good deal about the dream's waking context. This is a decided strength. Sometimes equivalent evidence can be gathered about a poem, as was the case with Rilke's sonnet. Such biographical information is frequently sketchy, though, and in any event is of a kind that critics are reluctant to use. It is an article of faith among critics, quite widely shared, that the text should stand alone, and that literary interpretation should as a result focus exclusively on the Work, ignoring the Life completely.

For millennia, it has been acknowledged that the dream uses as its raw materials the unresolved business of waking life. As Freud notes in his introductory chapters to *The Interpretation of Dreams*, the thread leads back from Maury – 'Nous rêvons de ce que nous avons vu, dit, désiré ou fait' – to Cicero – 'Then especially do the remnants of our waking thoughts and deeds move and stir within the soul.' Although he does not make much of it, Artemidorous distinguishes in the first section of his *Oneirocritica* between *oneiros*, the future state of affairs, and *enhypnion*, the present. Within the realm of the latter, he sees it as 'natural for a lover to seem to be with his beloved in a dream and for a frightened man to see what he fears'. More than 500 years earlier still, Herodotus, the father of history, tells of Xerxes, who, before setting out on his expedition against the Greeks, is advised by an old Persian dream interpreter that the visions that come to men in dreams are, for the most part, the thoughts of the day.[1]

The notion of the waking residue plays an important part in Freud's dream theory. It also appears as a component of most modern, 'bottom-up' theories of the dream, serving as the raw material from which a semantic salad is made. It is an idea with a lengthy pedigree, in other words; and is the second of the principles on which the present scheme rests. The assumption is that, in searching for an interpretative theme with which to make sense of a dream, its waking context is an excellent first resort. The waking, though not necessarily any more real than the sleeping, is a useful anchor and an admirable source of clues.

Here, two dreams serve as working examples, their aim to demonstrate the immediacy as well as the wealth of the connections that link sleeping to waking thought. The first, one of my own, is run-of-the-mill; the second special. My own is used not through any urge towards self-revelation, but because the details of its waking context can be established with a confidence that is often lacking in examples drawn from other people's books and articles, or from clinical practice; and also because, in the course of any study of dreams, the author should, as a matter of discipline, put his own head just once upon the slab. The second dream, categorically a weightier matter, both in itself and because of the contention that has grown up around it, is Freud's dream of Irma's injection. The one serves as groundwork and preparation for the other.

The day before my own dream occurred was largely taken up with drafting an earlier version of the present text: more specifically, with a preliminary attempt to describe experiences reported to me some weeks before by a gifted and highly successful engineer. In his eighties, he had claimed that he dreamt from time to time with the utmost vividness about works of art; impressionist paintings, modern sculptures, cartoons. These images were so clear that when he awoke he could start to sketch them: the cartoons, for example, he described as six drawings set out on a sheet of paper in two rows of three, each consisting of a creature part man, part insect. In the case of the impressionist paintings, he felt free to inspect them while still asleep as if they hung before him on a wall while he was awake. He recalled, too, that in his dream he drew someone else's attention to a brush-stroke that seemed to him especially fine.

Years after they had occurred, these dreams continued to baffle him, a sense he was happy to share. Why, he asked, having worked as an engineer all his life, and having had only a spectator's interest in the fine arts, should he have dreamt with such exceptional clarity and inventiveness about works of art, yet never dream with comparable clarity about machines? And why, if these extraordinary powers of invention are available to him, creating paintings, sculptures and cartoons out of thin air, could he not tap them for some more immediately useful purpose?

That night, like the engineer, I too dreamt with great clarity about works of art. These were displayed in a white-walled gallery, some hung on the wall in frames like paintings, others free-standing, like sculpture. They were works of technical virtuosity, assembled from interlocking pieces of wood, a cross between marquetry and jig-saw puzzles. Each piece in each work had been uniformly dyed a different colour. The ones hung like paintings were in low relief; those free-standing were fully three-dimensional. Both 'paintings' and 'sculptures' were entirely abstract. It was the paintings that caught the eye: their style was vigorous, even turbulent, but tightly constrained; Western, but at the same time Oriental, as if the work of a Chinese or Japanese who had lived for some time in the West.

While still in the gallery and finding my bearings, I was buttonholed by the artist, a tall Oriental woman who turned as we talked into the tennis player Martina Navratilova. I tried to explain to her that her works reminded me of the reliefs produced in the years after the First World War.[2] As I spoke, I became tongue-tied over the date '1918', twisting around it but failing to utter it. Her works, as I struggled, seemed almost to writhe.

This 'Navratilova' dream was characterised by a pervasive sense of ambiguity, as dreams often are: its 'paintings' both seemed to move and yet did not move; the artist was and was not Martina Navratilova; the gallery in which they were exhibited was both a gallery and something else unspecified – an old-fashioned bakery perhaps. Like the engineer's dreams, it was also inventive. At night, we had both been stocking the world with perceived entities – works of art – that had not previously been there. The thematic link between this dream and its waking context speaks for itself, and needs no labouring. This relationship with waking thought does have ramifications, however, and although inevitably more speculative, these also deserve to be mentioned.

It was, in the first place, a dream decidedly troubled in tone. There had been no anxiety attached, the engineer claimed, to his dreams about works of art. They were pleasurable. Where, then, does the air of anxiety and strain in my dream come from? The waking context has at least two sorts of answer to offer. The first is the anxiety attendant on any attempt to write something down for the first time, and to get it right. There had been no special difficulty in this respect, though, on the day in question; the description flowing, if anything, with more than usual fluency. One looks, therefore, for a further source, and finds it in the shape of a psychoanalytic report that I had read in the interstices of writing: one about a most unusual case, that of a deranged six-year-old girl who thought she was a boy.[3] She – or 'he' – suffered a foot fetish, slobbering over shoes in a distressing and erotic way. The child's therapy was long-drawn-out and only partially successful. The fetish disappeared. But, at the same time, the patient turned from a beautiful and radiant little 'boy', 'his' head teeming with trouble, into a relatively well-adjusted but plain little girl. The child's beauty, like her fetish, it seemed, had been a manifestation of her derangement.

The case study of the little girl centres on her transsexuality, and this is linked both to her beauty and to her neurotic symptoms. She produces neurotic symptoms when a 'boy', but these abate when she resumes her natural gender. The same three elements recur in the dream: the notions of gender, of beauty, and of an imaginatively inspired, neurotically driven, activity or product. The only actor other than myself is an artist who is also a woman of outstanding athleticism – a tennis star whose style on court is conspicuously male.[4] In the dream, the artist conveys a strong sense of personal accomplishment but seems dull. It is her works of art, rather than she herself, that radiate tension. It is as if the dream has taken the three key elements of the case study and juggled them round into a new permutation.

In the case study, each of these key elements undergoes a reversal in the course of psychotherapy. The little 'boy' is turned back into the little girl 'he' really is. Certain neurotic symptoms are expunged. And an aura of personal radiance or beauty disappears. These three changes capture just what one fears most about the costs and benefits of psychotherapy. A psyche that is driven and deranged, but is nevertheless in some sense brilliant, is exchanged for one that is stable and secure but also humdrum.

Grant this, and the Navratilova dream can be seen as possessing some of the qualities that structuralists ascribe to all dreams: it offers a better 'solution' to the little girl's plight. The notion of her transsexuality is retained, and stability is achieved by transferring her neurotic energy from the formation of a neurotic symptom, her foot fetish, to the fashioning of works of art – in which these self-same energies are embodied but contained.

Seen in this light, the dream implies a primitive species of argument, in dialectical form:

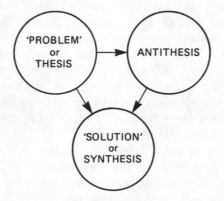

It starts with the beautiful little 'boy' who is deranged. It moves antithetically – via psychotherapy – to the little girl who is at least partially cured, but who is lacklustre. It then offers a 'solution' in the form of the adult artist and her works:

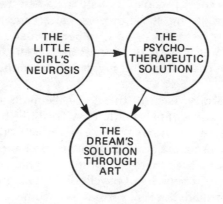

Transsexuality remains; personal magnetism is lost but is

replaced by a sense of accomplishment; and neurotic symptoms are removed in favour of works of art. Expanded diagrammatically, the dialectical movement is as follows:

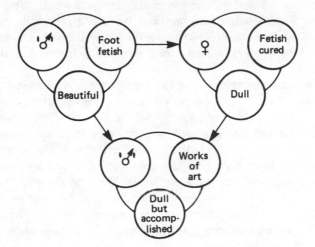

This may seem fanciful but, within its own limits, it is persuasive enough. There are at least three significant details in the Navratilova dream, though, that it leaves out of account. It says nothing about the form of the works of art themselves, so conspicuously a feature of the dream. It says nothing about the phrase over which I became tongue-tied: '1918'. And it gives no account of the dream's Oriental connotations.[5]

Help in making sense of these comes, again, from the task of drafting. For while superficially trouble-free, this contained, buried within it, certain tensions that were just beginning to make their presence felt. Rather than taking shape in the conventional way, with a narrative line, furnished with appropriate illustrations and examples, the text was one in which the illustrations and examples threatened to take charge, pushing all semblance of narrative out of the window. A war was joined, in other words, between conflicting methods of setting out the truth on the page. On the one hand, there is the story. This has a beginning, middle and end, and within it specific materials – dreams, poems, experiments – have a subservient part, being there to help the story along. On the other, the conventions of story-telling are abandoned. Specific materials are dominant, jostling against one another like nation states, and generating between them tensions that lie outside the author's control. Following one strategy, the psychologist spins a yarn, and runs the risk of trivialising his material by using it to illustrate a preordained scheme. Following the other, he allows his materials to speak for themselves, and runs the risk of an impression that is incoherent.[6]

This war can be typified in a variety of ways. One can speak, as Langer and Rycroft do, of discursive and non-discursive symbolism, or of the contrast between analytic and intuitive modes of thought. Among the grander and more sweepingly inclusive characterisations, one finds the distinction between Western and Oriental habits of thought, the one goal-directed and action-packed, the other more contemplative. There is also the distinction that puzzled my eminent engineer: the one between the technology that had made him so deservedly wealthy and, blooming in his sleeping mind's eye, the imagination that conjures up works of art.

Buried in the midst of these characterisations, there is the practical dilemma that faces the psychologist with a book or article to write: whether to put his faith in his storyline, or put it in his material. Although not fully alert to the fact at the time, it was just this dilemma that held me in its grip at the point when the Navratilova dream occurred. It could be seen as contributing to the dream's charge of anxiety, and also as furnishing it with some of its imagery. The 'paintings' in which the component parts fit together according to an abstract pattern rather than a narrative theme neatly captures the relationship between ideas in the non-discursive mode. The dream's Oriental details could well have signalled the importance of this mode too: the existence of a categorically less imperious approach to the handling of knowledge than that habitually employed. Even the date over which I had so gallingly stumbled – '1918' – slips neatly into place. It was the year, after all, in which a monstrously destructive conflict came to an end; a resolution, the dream suggests, that I was as yet in no position to bring about.

It is also worth noting that the two interpretative threads now teased out of the Navratilova dream and its waking context, although they appear quite unrelated, are in fact analogous. Both deal with the mechanisms of psychology as a professional activity: in the first instance, psychotherapy; in the second, the composition of a readily accessible psychological text. Both deal with the harm that psychologists can do in their professional capacities to human fabric on which their skills are imposed, the anxiety that the study of the mind can distort what is studied.

After all, then, the dream seems to be one of those that yields a central point of vantage: a proposition towards which all the various elements in the dream can be said to lead the gaze. One's footing on this vantage point is a little shaky, admittedly. All the more reason, therefore, to interpret the dream not in terms of this central proposition alone, but in terms, too, of the more detailed analyses on which it draws.

Before abandoning the Navratilova dream for weightier considerations, there is one last point that deserves to be made: it is about timing. The relevance of the dream's waking context, in the shape of the engineer's dream, was obvious more or less immediately upon waking. The existence of the link with the case study of the transsexual girl became apparent only more slowly, over the course of the next day or two, and then only in a rudimentary form: its full elaboration, as set out here, did not dawn for another two years. The same is true of the extent to which the dream epitomised the 'war' of methods implicit in psychological prose. When it first went to the publishers in draft form, this text still treated the Navratilova dream as demonstrating the importance of the waking context in a general way, but nothing more. A detailed interpretation was not attempted because the crucial connections had not been perceived.

Dream interpretation, this suggests, is in the nature of a gradually unfolding realisation. Doubtless, it is a process that can be hurried along by a sufficiently skilled and tactful interlocutor. Dawnings do seem to have their own rhythm, however, and it may be an error to hasten them too abruptly. If the dream is a communication, it is a communication, as Rycroft observes, from one aspect of a person to another aspect of that same person; a traffic in insights which the recipient – the person's waking self – is reluctant to acquire. Properly conducted, dream interpretation does not take the form of wisdom imposed from outside. Rather, it is an activity in which the interlocutor says to the dreamer only those things that the dreamer, 'were it not for resistance, could say of and to himself'. The dialogue between them is of an unusual kind, in that it consists of 'an actualisation of a potential intrapersonal dialogue'; the discovery of meaning takes place between two parts of one person, within a single head.[7]

Treating the Navratilova dream as groundwork, the time has come to talk again about Freud's dream of Irma's injection. It is one, as we have seen, to which Freud attached the greatest importance, seeing it as embodying the insight from which the whole body of psychoanalysis grew. In terms of its influence, it can claim to be one of the more momentous dreams in the history of our species; yet it remains baffling, as its many commentators have pointed out, because, as far as one can see, Freud's reading of it has so poor an anchorage either in the dream he reports or in the theory which he claimed subsequently to have built upon it.[8]

The comments made here about the Irma dream draw heavily on Kuper and Stone's illuminating paper.[9] While most reinterpreters, Erik Erikson for example, have accepted Freud's dream theory as substantially correct, and looked in the dream for evidence of the repressed sexual wishes that Freud's account omits, Kuper and Stone follow a different path. Attributing their method to the influence of Lévi-Strauss, they unpack the Irma dream as if it were a myth. Like myths, dreams are assumed to possess an internal structure in the form of an argument. This moves forward, step by step, attempting to reconcile or mediate opposites; it is a dialectic, in other words, that advances from an initial statement of a problem to a resolution. The problem itself is one posed by the anxieties dominating the dreamer's waking life at the time of the dream; and the resolution is a formulation that brings the elements of these waking anxieties into a state of equilibrium.

Kuper and Stone's procedure is one that accepts the dream as a text, places its faith in the waking context, and, like Jung, rejects the Freudian distinction between the dream's manifest and latent content. As Jung once put it,

'The "manifest" dream-picture is the dream itself and contains the whole meaning of the dream. When I find sugar in the urine, it is sugar and not just a façade for albumen. What Freud calls the "dream-façade" is the dream's obscurity, and this is really only a projection of our own lack of understanding. We say that the dream has a false front only because we fail to see into it. We would do better to say that we are dealing with something like a text that is unintelligible not because it has a façade – a text has no façade – but simply because we cannot read it.'[10]

Freud records the Irma dream in the following form:[11]

'Dream of July 23rd–24th, 1895
A large hall – numerous guests, whom we were receiving. – Among them was Irma. I at once took her on one side, as though to answer her letter and to reproach her for not having accepted my "solution" yet. I said to her: "If you still get pains, it's really only your fault". She replied: "If you only knew what pains I've got now in my throat and stomach and abdomen – it's choking me" – I was alarmed and looked at her. She looked pale and puffy. I thought to myself that after all I must be missing some organic trouble. I took her to the window and looked down her throat, and she showed signs of recalcitrance, like women with artificial dentures. I thought to myself that there was really no need for her to do that. – She then opened her mouth properly and on the right I found a big white patch; at another place I saw extensive whitish grey scabs upon some remarkable curly structures which were evidently modelled on the turbinal bones of the nose. – I at once called in Dr. M., and he repeated the examination and confirmed it. . . . Dr. M. looked quite different from usual; he was very pale, he walked with a limp and his chin was clean-shaven. . . . My friend Otto was now standing beside her as well, and my friend Leopold was percussing her through her bodice and saying: "She has a dull area low down on the left". He also indicated that a portion of the skin on the left shoulder was infiltrated. (I noticed this, just as he did, in spite of her dress.) . . . M. said "There's no doubt it's an infection, but no matter; dysentery will supervene and the toxin will be eliminated". . . . We were directly aware, too, of the origin of the infection. Not long before, when she was feeling unwell, my friend Otto had given her an injection

of a preparation of propyl, propyls . . . propionic acid . . .
trimethylamin (and I saw before me the formula for this printed
in heavy type). . . . Injections of that sort ought not to be made
so thoughtlessly. . . . And probably the syringe had not been
clean.'

Freud establishes that the young woman, Irma, is a family friend,
a widow, and also a patient of his. Otto is a colleague who had
been staying with Irma and reported to Freud that she was still
not recovered. Freud detected, he says, a note of reproof in Otto's
comments, and that night had prepared a case history of Irma's
treatment for a senior colleague, Dr M., in order to justify
himself. He concludes that his dream is in the nature of a 'plea',
reminiscent of the excuses offered by a man accused of borrowing
a kettle and returning it damaged: 'The defendant asserted first,
that he had given it back undamaged; secondly, that the kettle
had a hole in it when he borrowed it; and thirdly, that he had
never borrowed a kettle from his neighbour at all.' He also
concludes that Otto's remarks about Irma had annoyed him, and
that he took revenge by making the fault for Irma's illness his.
The dream, in short, represented 'a particular state of affairs as I
should have wished it to be'. Its 'content was the fulfilment of a
wish and its motive was a wish'.[12]

The oddity of this conclusion, of course, in the light of the
profound significance that Freud attributes to the Irma dream, is
that the dream omits all mention of sex, and his interpretation of
it introduces sex only in a relatively marginal way. Yet without
that additional element, it is a conclusion that could as easily have
been reached forty years earlier by Wilhelm Griesinger –
Griesinger having maintained, as Freud knew and acknowledged, that dreams shared with psychoses the common feature
of being 'the imaginary fulfilment of wishes', a point taken up
and elaborated by Freud's own teacher in psychiatry, Meynert.[13]

Freud admits that there are points at which the dream baffles
him: 'There is at least one spot in every dream at which it is
unplumbable – a navel, as it were, that is its point of contact with
the unknown.' In this case, bafflement centred on Irma's
complaint of abdominal pains. By association, he links these
pains to his wife's thrombosis in the course of a previous
pregnancy. It also inspires a startling footnote, introduced in 1909

and not removed until 1925, in which he suggests that this detail is prophetic: 'my patient's "unsolved" gastric pains, for which I was so anxious not to be blamed, turned out to be the forerunners of a serious disorder caused by gall-stones.' It was a long time before he realised quite how bizarre his proposal must seem: that a physician's dream could predict the development in a patient, supposedly suffering from hysterical anxiety, of some quite new abdominal disease.[14]

As well as confessing bafflement, Freud is also explicit about the fact that his interpretation is incomplete: 'I will not pretend that I have completely uncovered the meaning of this dream or that its interpretation is without a gap. . . . I myself know the points from which further trains of thought could be followed.' Recent scholarship indicates rather precisely where that gap is to be found. It also demonstrates a lack of candour on Freud's part that amounts to intellectual dishonesty.[15]

Irma – in real life, Emma – had in fact been examined by Freud's friend Fliess, to see whether gastric pains, which Freud had assumed to be hysterical in origin, might be of 'nasal origin'. Fliess, it should be said, was an ear, nose and throat specialist from Berlin, who held bizarre views about the relation of the turbinal bones in the nose to the female sexual organs. At Freud's instigation, he not merely examined Emma, but performed an operation that included draining a sinus cavity. By accident, he left a large piece of gauze in her sinus. In time, this putrified, and when removed gave rise to a copious haemorrhage. Freud, who was present, is said almost to have fainted. A month later, there was still so much bleeding that the ligation of the carotid artery was considered. In April, he wrote to Fliess: 'Gloomy times, unbelievably gloomy. Mainly this business with Emma, which is rapidly deteriorating'. The while, Fliess was proving himself to be an awkward colleague. He demanded formal retractions at the least hint of criticism, and later was in a position to insist on the deletion of any material in *The Interpretation of Dreams* that he found professionally compromising.

In the spring and summer of 1895 Freud had on his hands a bungled operation for which he was professionally responsible, and that could turn at any minute into a scandal. At the same time, he was attempting a most ambitious piece of theorising: his *Project for a Scientific Psychology*, completed in the same year. At the heart of this endeavour, vitally significant to Freud, although overshadowed since by his more recognisably psychoanalytic works, was an effort to reconcile the events in the mind with events in the brain. Such reconciliations, as he found, are extraordinarily difficult to achieve – not just for reasons of factual ignorance, but for philosophical reasons too.[16]

Inspection of his dream suggests that, in the course of it, Freud moves from a completely self-deceptive view of the Irma operation to the admission that something has gone wrong. At the same time he advances from a naively psychological view of the relation between Irma's mental state and her symptoms towards a more sophisticated one. Kuper and Stone plot this movement in a form that should by now be familiar. It is this:

'PROBLEM'

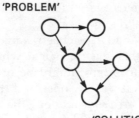

'SOLUTION'

Expanded to accommodate the fact that each step in the dream's argument consists of a story with more than one element, the format looks like this:

'PROBLEM'

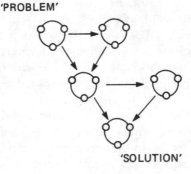

'SOLUTION'

108

The dream's initial statement, Kuper and Stone say, consists of three claims. These are linked together:

(i) Irma's illness is sexual and hysterical in origin, organic in symptoms;
(ii) it is caused by Irma, and is her fault;
(iii) in choking, she is voluntarily refusing to speak.

There follows the dream's first antithetical step, a story equally coherent but quite different:

(i) her illness is organic in origin, hysterical in symptoms;
(ii) it is neglected by the doctor;
(iii) her resistance, in choking, is involuntary.

Three more steps lead to the dream's conclusion:

(i) Irma's illness is organic, sexual *and* hysterical;
(ii) it is caused by a careless doctor; and,
(iii) it gives rise not to choking but to dysentery.

To the reader who has access only to the text of the dream itself, the mention of sexuality in two of these three stories must come as a surprise. The text makes no reference to sex at all. While many psychoanalytic commentators introduce sexuality to their readings as a matter of course, Kuper and Stone are more circumspect: 'From a structural perspective, the resolution of the dream is a resolution of the dialectic progression. At last the real etiology of Irma's illness is discovered. The disease is caused (1) by an injection of toxic substances (2) with a dirty syringe (3) by a thoughtless doctor, Otto. Each of these three statements is filled with double meanings' – and those double meanings are sexual.

The German original makes it clear, apparently, that the idea of an injection has, for Freud, a sexual overtone: Irma's trouble is traced to her contact with Otto's dirty 'squirter' (*Spritze*); and one of the dream's toxic substances, trimethylamin, was believed by

Fliess, as Freud states, to be a product of 'sexual metabolism'. For Freud, sex was at that time the key to the synthesis that his *Project* sought to achieve: it linked the physical to the psychic, and did so in a remarkably literal way. Faulty sexual practices led, Freud believed, to a kind of self-poisoning, chemicals emanating from the sexual organs proving toxic, and leading both to anxiety and to the formation of neurotic symptoms. Kuper and Stone conclude, accordingly, that if the Irma dream is read in the light of Freud's current theoretical preoccupations, it not only shelves the problem of Emma, but convinces Freud that his synthesis is correct. Both hysterical symptoms and dreams are the consequences of sexual chemicals that have gone astray. When Otto injects Irma, he is displaying his sexual carelessness: a thoughtless man who causes anxiety neurosis in a woman by arousing in her desires that are not fulfilled.

While accepting that these ambiguities of sexual meaning could well have been obvious to Freud, a sense of awkwardness remains. To show that the Irma dream contains sexual symbolism is one thing; to show that it expresses a repressed sexual wish is quite another. Either one accepts the dream for what it appears to be: that of a professional under fire – urgently wishing to be in the right or, if there is to be a débâcle, to emerge from it blame-free. Or one attempts to explain the significance that Freud accorded it: a revelation of the sexual needs that all dreams were held to fulfil. To do that, one must learn more about the man himself.

At the heart of the Irma dream is a medical mistake, Otto's use of a dirty syringe, and close to the heart of Freud's anxieties as he fell asleep must have been thoughts about the bungled operation that Fliess had carried out on Emma's nose. In his dream, Freud shifts the burden of responsibility from his own shoulders and Fliess's onto those of a younger colleague, Otto. Otto's error, moreover, is seen as one of carelessness rather than misinformation. The Irma dream thus shows shows every sign of being an exercise in bad faith. Certainly it is less than half-way to acknowledging what had to be acknowledged: that Fliess held views that were in part at least those of a crackpot – not just about the sexual significance of the turbinal bones in the nose, but his obsessive concern, too, with periodicity, a 23-day cycle in the lives of men and a 28-day one in the lives of women.

Historians seem agreed that Freud's dependence on Fliess was at this point extreme. Within a year of Emma's misfortunes at Fliess's hands, he allowed Fliess to remove parts of his own turbinal bone – and he underwent this operation on grounds that reveal the degree of his commitment. He believed that arrhythmia of the heart, from which he was then suffering, could prove to be nasal in origin. Such was his trust in Fliess's periodicity theories that, in 1898, he bestowed on his friend the title 'the Kepler of biology'. And even when they fell out, as they did two years later over Freud's pre-emption of another of Fliess's ideas, that of bisexuality, he continued to use Fliess's ideas in a remarkably uncritical way.[17]

All this one can say while taking the Irma dream at face value, but it does not in the least account for the sense of illumination – of deep secrets revealed – that Freud attached to it. To do that, one must look elsewhere. As it happens, Freud passed two significant landmarks at just the point in his life when the illuminative force of his Irma dream was dawning upon him. In 1896, his father died; and in 1897, while still only forty-one, he ceased to have sexual relations with his wife. Freud's sexual intimacies with Martha ceased, it is said, because he found the methods of birth control then available distasteful: it is unfortunate, he thought, that 'all the devices hitherto invented for preventing conception impair sexual enjoyment, hurt the finer susceptibilities of both partners and even actually cause illness.'[18] There seems to have been a diminution of desire if not actual impotence. In 1897, he wrote to Fliess: 'sexual excitation is of no more use to a person like me.'

A later conversation with Emma Jung suggests that Freud, having had six children with Martha, regarded his marriage to her as 'amortised'. Certainly the attentive if untrustworthy Ernest Jones seems to have assumed that the diminution of Freud's sexual desire was related to a fear of old age and death – a death that, in his own case, Freud believed was going to strike early, having been persuaded by Fliess's calculation that his life was destined to end at the age of fifty-one. The death of his own father could also have had a bearing. Freud once spoke of a man who 'was the most pronounced rebel imaginable . . . on the other hand, at a deeper level he was still the most submissive of sons, who after his father's death denied himself all enjoyment of women out of a tender sense of guilt.' In this allusion, he could

111

well have been speaking obliquely about himself.

Whatever the cause, and there may well have been several, Freud's sexual relations with Martha ceased more or less precisely at the point in his life when his self-analysis began, and he launched himself convincedly into the psychological theories for which he is now known. As Roazen remarks, it seems likely that Freud's libidinal energies were transferred into theoretical construction.

If one accepts the necessity of finding some source, within the Irma dream, for Freud's sense of profound illumination, and if one also accepts that this source ought to have some detectable bearing on the sexual theory that Freud was subsequently to develop on the dream's strength, then one is forced to look again at its resolution: Otto's careless use of his dirty 'squirter'.

The dirty 'squirter', it surely is not too far-fetched to suggest, could well have been Freud's. The responsibility for its use is one that, in the course of his dream, he passes to the younger and still virile Otto. The sense of revelation that Freud attached to the Irma dream then at last begins to make sense. It centres on two discoveries. The first is that the burden of sustaining a sexual relationship with Martha is one from which he can step free. The second is that the very constituents of this burden, the turmoil of sex and guilt, instinctual energy and repression, can be turned into theory. The noxious sexual chemicals that he feared had been set loose in his own central nervous system and Martha's by the unsatisfactory nature of their coupling could now be contained. Henceforth, they were to be the elements of a theoretical construction, an ivory tower of truth, in which the dangers of the instinctual life were permanently controlled.

Again, a dream and its waking context yield, not a single interpretation, but two, and they coexist. The Irma dream concerns the anxieties of professional life. In it, Freud evades a professional responsibility, and places it, not on Fliess, where at least in part it belongs, but on someone both junior and quite innocent. It is also a dream about the ways in which the stresses and strains of the marriage bed in the apartment at 19 Berggasse could be metamorphosed into theory, pure and eternal.

The repressed sexual wish that the Irma dream expresses is revealed not as a lustful craving for some forbidden object – his sister-in-law Minna, say – but as a stifled longing to be free from the carnal side of sexuality, and to experience once again, to re-use Farrell's turns of phrase, those images of 'piercing tender-ness', of 'purity and love without limit', that are hidden by the dross of tainted circumstances, but are still capable of ringing through our minds 'like the chime of a bell on a frosty morning'.[19] Paradoxically, it was in Freud's case not lust that had been repressed, but a longing to be without it.

If it is a dream that poses and then answers a problem, as Kuper and Stone's structural analysis insists it must, then the Irma dream is adaptive in two interesting respects.[20] It shows, if he is a psychologist, what manoeuvres at the level of the imagination a passionate theoretician must find it natural to engage in. In-tuitively, automatically, if he is to stay in play, he must be able to disown his errors as a matter of course; and he must discover how to escape from the exigencies of private life by turning them into ideas, the bricks from which theory is built.

Notes

(1) Strachey (1954), p. 8.

(2) I had in mind the works of Jean Arp.

(3) Hopkins (1984).

(4) The tennis star in question is known to me only as a figment on television. About her character or personal life, I know nothing. She is linked to the notion of transsexuality quite directly in that, at the time, her coach was Dr Renée Richards, the male tennis player who changed sex. Evidence of my own interest in issues of sex and gender is to be found in *Bodies of Knowledge*, published in the year that the Navratilova dream occurred.

(5) It can sensibly be argued that Martina Navratilova's appearance is in certain respects Oriental: her high cheek-bones, for example. In the interests of completeness, it should be added that my wife and mother are both painters; that the former is somewhat Oriental in appearance and the latter is known by a masculine nickname; also that Navrati-lova, like myself, is left-handed. The dream's Oriental connotations can be seen, too, as having a prospective significance. A few months later, I bought three eighteenth-

century Japanese prints, something that at any previous moment in my life it would not have crossed my mind to do. The birth of such enthusiasms, and the extent to which they may be anticipated in dreams, is a topic about which psychology has in the past been silent.

(6) A surging narrative energy is the hallmark of pulp fiction. The truth is another matter. In the presentation of non-fictional material, it is unclear where the distinction between narrative and explanation lies. Scientists' idiomatic use of the word 'story' to embrace arguments and explanations suggests that, in practice, such distinctions can be blurred. This scarcely seems satisfactory, though. A radical solution to the awkwardness is the one adopted by Barthes in *A Lover's Discourse* (1979). There, he arranges his material alphabetically. It may be that psychology's first great achievement, its Copernican revolution, will consist not in a factual discovery about the mind, nor in a new theory about it, but in the establishment of an 'abstract' style: the equivalent in psychological prose of those styles in paintings in which story-telling and literary allusion play no part.

(7) Rycroft (1979), p. 60.

(8) Ibid., p. 29; Sulloway (1979), p. 327.

(9) Kuper and Stone (1982); also Kuper (1983).

(10) Storr (1983), p. 177. In practice, there is not one 'structural' approach to the dream, but several. Foulkes (1978), for example, retains both free association and the distinction between manifest and latent content. The structural method used by Kuper and Stone differs from the 'hermeneutic' one adopted here in two respects at least. Not only does the structuralist assume that each dream has a quasi-logical structure; as a matter of course, he also invokes transformational codes: in this case, a code whereby the sleeping Freud translates psychological states into the physical symptoms that the Irma dream actually contains. In the context of Freud's preoccupations with hysteria, this is a perfectly reasonable step, but also a somewhat risky one, in that it opens the way for argument about the merits of competing codes.

(11) Here I use Strachey's (1954) translation. The Irma dream is mentioned in the *Project*, but was not published fully until

five years later. Like Darwin's insight into the evolutionary significance of the Galapagos finches, Freud's awareness of the Irma dream's importance seems to have grown only slowly: Sulloway (1982). Freud's hagiographers, among them Ernest Jones, place the turning-point in the autumn of 1897, when Freud undertook his 'heroic' self-analysis. Sulloway argues convincingly for a dawning that was more gradual and one heavily dependent on the insight of others: Sulloway (1979), p. 327.

(12) Strachey (1954), p. 118.

(13) Sulloway (1979), p. 324.

(14) Strachey (1954), pp. 111 and 116. For those interested in the origins of eloquence, it is worth noting that a memorable phrase – that about the dream's 'navel' – should have been inspired by the need for a cover-up.

(15) In fact, the relevant historical information seems to have been available for quite a long time: it would seem that Schur published it in 1966. It has been assimilated only gradually, however. Kuper and Stone (1982) give details.

(16) See Sulloway (1979) for an account of Freud's career as a laboratory scientist, and of the influence of this experience on his subsequent theorising.

(17) Sulloway (1979) provides a sympathetic and exhaustively thorough account of Fliess's views and their influence on Freud.

(18) Roazen (1975), pp. 49–55.

(19) Farrell (1978), p. 215.

(20) The notion of the dream as an adaptive or, more specifically, as a problem-solving device has gained considerable support among the scientifically inclined: see, e.g., the discussion in Foulkes (1978). It resurfaces at points throughout the rest of this text.

CHAPTER NINE

Older Residues

If the dream is read as a poem, as Richter's insight suggests, and if the dream's waking context is treated as the interpreter's first resort – if dream and waking context are treated for this purpose as parts of a single fabric – the rudiments of an interpretative scheme are already in place. What emerges, characteristically, is not an unequivocal reading of a text that is confused or corrupted, but one in which two or more systems of meaning coexist and may interact. Conceptually, the task is complex; and it will frequently lead to areas of indeterminacy. But it need be neither sloppy nor vague.

As it stands, the scheme is excessively cautious, though. Not all the unresolved anxieties and tensions of the dream's waking context are immediately apparent. Others are 'older', hidden. In attempting to characterise these, two specific possibilities will be canvassed: that dreams can tap more deeply seated residues, in the form of alternative systems of self; and that, beyond these residues, which are personal to the individual, there could also exist regularities of experience that influence all individuals equally, some specific to a given culture, others present largely irrespective of culture.

The terrain is a dangerous one, because the model of the mind most appropriate to such discussion will strike some readers as 'Jungian'. As a matter of principle, the present argument is designed to avoid all mention of the occult and supernatural, the cast of mind that has earned Jung a bad name. His view possesses virtues, nonetheless, and it seems prudent to cherish these: notably, those that allow for the partitioning of experience between the avowed and unavowed; that lead one to expect, hidden beneath an avowed pattern of belief or desire, its opposite – a species of antiphony or counterpoint; and that take seriously the existence of a substratum of experience to which all human beings have intuitive access.

The pattern of psychic organisation that Jung's categories suggest is one built on mirror images, reversals and transpositions. Within the mind-set of the mechanical or communications engineer, this is less than easy to grasp. It is perfectly plain, though, in the pattern-making traditions of cultures less dissociatedly instrumental than our own. One sees these principles incorporated, for example, into the medallions or *guls* that Afghan tribesmen still weave into their rugs:

In this design, there is mirroring, the reversal of values and spatial transposition. The left-hand half of this particular *gul* is a mirror image of the right-hand half, but the values are reversed: dark becomes light and light becomes dark. At first glance, the bottom half of the design may seem to mirror the top half, but a second glance shows that this is not so. Dark and light again are reversed, but here the elements in the design are transposed. Where, in the top half, the star is above the dog-like beast, in the bottom half it is the dog-like beast that is above the star. As with *guls* in Afghan rugs, so – Jung's categories imply – with the internal organisation of the mind. (The highly conventionalised pattern of the dog refers us, incidentally, not only to the living dog, but also to certain more abstract ideas. In this context, the dog is a talisman that drives away all undesirables including witches, robbers and diseases.)

As a working example, take a particular dream – or, in this case, a set of dreams: those of the great nineteenth-century critic and arbiter of taste, John Ruskin. As he grew older, Ruskin was plagued increasingly with dreams about snakes. Being an exhaustively copious and unguarded chronicler of his own states of mind, he provides us with a clear record of what those dreams were like. He seems first to have noted that he was experiencing sexual nightmares of young girls when he was in his late forties: 'singularly unclean, disgusting, ludicrous'. On 14 August 1867, he writes that he is trying to conquer these base dreams, but fails. On 9 March of the next year, he dreams that he is showing his young cousin Joan a snake and making her feel its scales: 'Then she made me feel it, and it became a fat thing, like a leech, and adhered to my hands, so that I could hardly pull it off.'[1]

In November of the same year, 1868, he notes that his serpent dreams seemed to have abated. But twelve months later, on 1 November 1869, he records:

'the most horrible serpent dream I ever had yet in my life. The deadliest came out into the room under a door. It rose up like a Cobra – with horrible round eyes and had woman's, or at least Medusa's, breasts. It was coming after me . . . but I got some pieces of marble off a table and threw at it, and that cowed it and it went back; but another small one fastened on my neck like a leech, and nothing would pull it off.'

Ten years after first suffering his serpent dreams, Ruskin suffered a grotesque hallucination of 'the Evil One'. He wrestled throughout the night and was discovered naked and insane the next morning. For weeks he remained in a state of wild delirium from which he was never fully to recover.

By this time, now in his late fifties, Ruskin had entered a condition in which clear boundaries between waking and sleeping thought were dissolving. The decade of the 1870s, as his biographer Rosenberg says, became an unavailing struggle to preserve his sanity. From his pen, there flowed meanwhile the extraordinary invective of *Fors Clavigera*, published monthly from 1871 onwards, in the form of 'Letters to the Workmen and Labourers of Great Britain'. More than half a million words in length, it records Ruskin's pilgrimage through the squalor of modern industrial Europe and his yearning for an unsoiled and idealised past. The tone and energy of *Fors Clavigera* are themselves hallucinatory, and chronicle a path that Ruskin himself was treading along the brink of derangement:

'But for us of the old race – few of us now left, – children who reverence our fathers, and are ashamed of ourselves; comfortless enough in that shame, and yearning for one word or glance from the graves of old, yet knowing ourselves to be of the same blood, and recognising in our hearts the same passions, with the ancient masters of humanity; – we, who feel as men, and not as carnivorous worms; we, who are every day recognising some inaccessible height of thought and power, and are miserable in our shortcomings, – the few of us now standing here and there, alone, in the midst of this yelping, carnivorous crowd, mad for money and lust, tearing each other to pieces, and starving each other to death, and leaving heaps of their dung and ponds of their spittle on every palace floor and altar stone, – it is impossible for us, except in the labour of our hands, not to go mad.'[2]

A sense of malevolence immerses Ruskin, at first intermittently and then more continuously. At one point he likens Britannia, Empress of the Seas, to a 'slimy polype, multiplying by involuntary vivisection, and dropping half putrid pieces of itself wherever it crawls or contracts', a passage all the more dream-like for beginning with an elaborate recipe for Yorkshire Goose Pie.[3] The weather, particularly, serves Ruskin as an extension of his own condition. In 1879, for example, he describes a storm at his home at Brantwood:

'the air one loathsome mass of sultry and foul fog, like smoke . . . terrific double streams of reddish-violet fire, not forked or zig-zag, but rippled rivulets – two at the same instant . . . lasting on the eye at least half a second, with grand artillery-peals following. . . . While I have written this sentence the cloud has again dissolved itself, like a nasty solution in a bottle, with miraculous and unnatural rapidity. . . . Three times light and three times dark since last I wrote, and the darkness seeming each time as it settles more loathsome. . . . One lurid gleam of white cumulus in upper lead-blue sky, seen for half a minute through the sulphurous chimney-pot vomit of blackguardly cloud beneath.'[4]

Periods of lucidity were to return, and in the course of one he wrote the reflections on the *Cathedral at Amiens* that were to serve as inspiration to Proust. It was from Ruskin's recreation of an idealised past that Proust's recreation of his own past in *À la Recherche du Temps Perdu* grew. Ruskin's equilibrium was destroyed, though. Physically there was no longer firm ground on which he could steady himself. Repeatedly, surges of madness engulfed him. The periods of lucidity became briefer; and by his sixties Ruskin had irrevocably lost his way.

In the spirit of the last chapter, there are a number of down-to-earth remarks that can be made about Ruskin's madness and the part played in it by his dreams of snakes. The waking context is obvious; pathetically so. At the time of the dreams' first onset, he had recently proposed marriage to Rose La Touche, whom he had fallen helplessly in love with when she was still a child. Now more nearly adult, she stalled, asking for more time, but in the end rejected him and castigated him, too, for his loss of religious faith. More and more a zealot, Rose lost her own reason, and she died a few years later, in 1875, leaving Ruskin inconsolable.

More generally, Ruskin was obsessed with the purity of pre-adolescent girls like Rose, and was horrified at the prospect of their sexual maturity. Accordingly, the snakes in his dreams must be seen as emblematic of adult sexuality. As in the garden of Eden, they also represent the Devil incarnate. No mere commentary upon his passion for Rose, they made painfully explicit its hidden carnal component. The effect of this self-revelation was to unhinge him; and it was in the course of one of these hallucinatory episodes – half dream, half waking nightmare – that he first became insane.

Interesting puzzles remain, of course. In the dream recorded on 1 November 1869, he manages to cow the large Medusa snake with women's breasts, but a smaller one attaches itself to his own neck, and it is this that he cannot pull off. Why a snake with breasts? Medusa, after all, was famous for having snakes instead of hair, and eyes that turned men to stone, but her breasts have no special mythological significance. Why was it a smaller snake that attached itself to Ruskin's neck, and could not be pulled off? And why his neck?

These loose ends aside, Ruskin's snake dreams do seem at first sight to fit quite comfortably within the rather constricting frame of reference that the last chapter provides. But on reflection, other doubts are raised. The common-sense explanation of Ruskin's horror is that he was guilt-ridden about sex because brought up in a regime of intense Evangelical piety. Whatever is sexual in such a context must be evil, and whatever evil, sexual. In one respect this explanation satisfies; in another, it does not. Ruskin's upbringing was intensely puritanical, and he did remain locked, throughout his life, within a frame of mind that was inexorably high-minded. On the other hand, he seems to have spoken forthrightly about his own sexuality as an adult, and in a spirit that does not in the least conform to our notions of Victorian piety. Rosenberg comments that in his forties he wrote 'an astonishingly candid' letter to a female friend, Mrs William Cowper, about the sin he saw himself as sharing with Rousseau: that of autoeroticism.

Altogether more disturbing to Ruskin than sex itself was the prospect of the female body in its mature form. Convention holds that he was horrified into impotence on his wedding night by discovering – as the two young Englishmen in Farrell's novel had discovered – that women have pubic hair. Whether or not this story is literally true, there is no question that his marriage to Effie Gray was unconsummated, and that the reluctance lay not with Effie but with him. Nor is there any doubt that his desires were directed, as he grew older, to ever younger girls. Where his first love, Adele Domecq, was seventeen at the time of his devotion to her, Rose La Touche was only twelve.

The physical changes wrought by puberty in Rose were ones that Ruskin saw as tragic. 'I shall not see her till November,' he wrote when she was thirteen. 'Nay, I shall never see *her* again. It's another Rosie every six months now. Do I want to keep her from growing up? Of course I do.' Yet, in the year that he first met Rose La Touche and conceived a passion for her – as overwhelming, he was later to say, as had been his passion for Turner's paintings – he had also experienced a carnal awakening in Italy. This occurred in the presence of a painting by Veronese, whom he praised for his 'magnificent animality'. Deeply disturbed by this eruption of a desire that he could neither express nor deny, he contemplated going to Venice or to Paris 'and doing I don't know

121

what'. Instead, he had settled for his role as uncle to the pre-adolescent girls of the school at Winnington Hall.

The opposition of his chaste passion for the fair-haired Rose to the life of the flesh could not have been more precisely poised, for while discovering Veronese's animality, he also spied – and was seized by – the spectacle of a half-naked, ten-year-old Italian girl, as dark as Rose was fair, lying bare-limbed on a heap of sand.

It must follow that Ruskin was not engaged in a comprehensive sexual repression, but was trapped, rather, between two paths, two repertoires of desire, neither of which was to prove enduringly stable or satisfying. His pursuit of Rose, the path he avowed, was doomed to frustration. He followed it with such avidity, perhaps, for that very reason. The alternative, that of the child prostitutes of Paris and of doing with them he knew not what, was socially prohibited; but even if it had not been, it would presumably have generated within him more conflict than he could have known how to endure.

The conventional solution to the interpretative problem that Ruskin's snakes pose is to talk about phallic symbols. Certainly, his snakes do seem to have phallic significance; but to point to their symbolism is not to explain why they plagued Ruskin as they did. One needs, rather, a language with which to describe a system within which needs that seem naturally to belong together can become split apart, and then act upon one another in dangerous and disruptive ways. If Ruskin had had the benefits of a progressive twentieth-century upbringing, the animal vitality he perceived in Veronese and the high-minded longing he felt for Rose could perhaps have been gathered up within a single 'mature' relationship with a woman more nearly his own age. Alternatively, he could have entered into two quite different sorts of sexual intimacy one after the other. He could have enjoyed both 'Miss Fair' and 'Miss Dark', either as different individuals, or as different facets of the same individual. If, on the other hand, he had been capable of such easy pleasures, the problem, presumably, would not have arisen in the first place: neither Veronese nor Rose La Touche would have electrified him in quite the way they did.

In Jung, we find the outlines of the model we need. His notions of persona, anima, animus and shadow all serve to segregate or partition conflicting demands made upon the individual and to maintain the psychic system as a whole within a state of equilibrium. The dream, too, is seen as contributing to the system's equilibrium and as being essentially compensatory in function. Also helpful is his assumption that compensatory relationships exist between the components within his model: between the mask-like persona that we each display to the world, for example, and the anima or animus that is unacknowledged but that makes its presence felt in our apparently arbitrary and stereotyped passions and predilections.[5]

When such a model is applied to a life like Ruskin's, however, it does not fully alert us to what we find: two patterns or repertoires of self, each embodying passionately felt but antithetical needs, one at war with the other. Like the components of a multiple personality, the halves of Ruskin's life did battle: the Fair seeming to vanquish the Dark, but the Dark returning in his dreams and leading in the end to chaotic dissolution.

It is at this point that diagrams come to one's aid. Sexuality in each of us can be seen as a series of choices or decisions: the choice made on our behalf by our genes and chromosomes, determining whether we are going to live inside a male body or a female one; the choice made for us – inadvertently, it seems, by our mothers – determining whether we will perceive ourselves, at heart, as essentially male or female; the choice, also made early in life and equally mysterious, determining whether we will be erotically attracted to those of the opposite sex or those of our own sex; and so on. Such choices look like a tree in which the branches overlap, each decision creating a new layer of branches:[6]

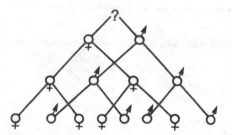

The point about such trees, in the present context, is that they can be used to generate residual paths. A particular man may be male, biologically speaking; he may see himself a male, but find that he is drawn towards members of his own sex. His path through the decision tree will look like this:

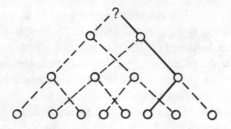

Some of his choices, however, may have been made with difficulty, or be for some other reason precarious. If that is so, residual paths will exist, alternative repertoires of identity and need, that, at some later point in his life, he may find himself tempted or indeed compelled to explore. One insecure choice within such a tree can beget another, so several residual paths can establish themselves side by side. And the larger the tree grows, with the addition of further layers to represent other sex-linked choices – social manner, occupation, dress, and so on – the more scope these residual paths will have for proliferation. If, in the present example, the second choice, that of gender identity, is insecure, two residual paths establish themselves automatically: (i) the path that leads the man in question to be someone who sees himself as at heart female, and is attracted to other men; and (ii) the path that leads him to be a man who sees himself as female, but is drawn to women:

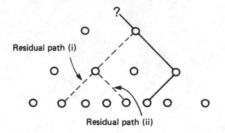

What is at issue in such diagrams as these is not the Unconscious as traditionally conceived – as it appears, say, in Freud's dream theory. These residual paths may well be ones that the individual in question is half willing to entertain in the form of sexual reveries or fantasies, or in his choice of jokes; or to acknowledge more obliquely in the form of idiosyncrasies of taste or social mannerism that are subtly out of keeping with the path to which he is explicitly committed. They nonetheless remain in the margin of his way of life as it is explicitly constituted, and as such are precisely the kind of material on which, when dreaming, his imagination will tend to feed. In terms of behaviour that is explicitly avowed, the movement from one path to another may never occur, or at the other extreme it can take catastrophic form: an apparently happily married man with two children and a mortgage can find himself driven to abandon hearth and home in favour of life in a bed-sitting-room with a homosexual youth less than half his age, and without a virtue to recommend him. Our attachments and revulsions, it would seem to follow, depend in essence not on who the other person is, but on the system of self that he or she enables us to occupy or prevents us from occupying. The experience of falling in love is the discovery that another person enables us to inhabit a self, much as we might a house; love of a more enduring kind is the knowledge that, without that person, there would be no such house; and the possessive rages with which love is surrounded are our attempts, when threatened, to keep that house intact and keep it for ourselves.

These residual paths arise, of course, in other areas of experience besides that of sexuality: that of aggression, for instance. They represent not the 'true self' of the individual in question, but alternative selves – there, in the margins of behaviour that is avowed, and contrary to it. If, in turn, they themselves become explicit, they may prove no more stable or satisfying than the paths they replace. By their very occurrence, they may make it impossible to return to the original path, leaving the individual in question marooned. As a consequence, a stable way of life depends on internal negotiations that may be as tortuous as they are prolonged. The tragedy of Ruskin's life lay in his discovery that negotiation was in the end impossible. Dark and Fair refused either to go away or to be reconciled; and his snake dreams haunted him loathsomely as a result. If, on the other hand, negotiation had been possible, he could scarcely have written as he did. And if he had not written, one of the most

125

fertile chains of intellectual influence of the last century or so, connecting Ruskin not only to Proust but to socialists like William Morris and Clement Attlee, and to more visionary reformers like Gandhi, would not have come about.

Why snakes though? Is it enough to imply that there is a symbolic tendency within each head which spontaneously equates 'snake' with 'penis'? As Freud and Jung unite in remarking, dreams frequently reveal 'archaic remnants'; ideas, that is to say, whose 'presence cannot be explained by anything in the individual's own life and which seem to be aboriginal, innate, and inherited shapes of the human mind'.[7] To the scientifically inclined, it seems inconceivable that specific images, like that of the snake, should be genetically encoded and transmitted in the way, say, that the shape of the human nose is. The fact remains that snakes are a remarkably common image in the dreams not only of those who have good reason to be scared of snakes, but those who have had no everyday dealings with them.

What is one to say? Two interpretative avenues beckon: one common-sensical, the other altogether more a question of speculation. Common sense treats archetypal images like the snake, in dreams and myths alike, as abstractions based on a common stockpile of shared experience: that of growing up and growing old in a human body, male or female; of family life and intimate attachment; of emotions like desire, jealousy and depression; also, more specifically, of knowledge of the evocative symbols around which the life of a particular culture is constructed. On this argument, Ruskin dreamt of snakes because he had learnt at his mother's knee that is was the Devil in the form of a serpent who offered naked Adam and naked Eve an apple from the tree of the knowledge of good and evil. We know that he was an exceptionally solitary boy, obsessed with the visual: he may have dwelt, alone in his room, on specific images of nakedness and snakes, illustrative of this particular Biblical theme.

This line of explanation, persuasive in itself, does not illuminate the exceptional emotional charge with which the image of the snake was invested in Ruskin's adult mind. To do that, one might move, psychoanalytically speaking, into deeper waters. One could argue that it is not the snake as such that is frightening, but the snake-as-penis; and not penises in a general way, but more specifically the fantasy of the father's penis as it enters the mother's body in the enactment of the Primal Scene, or sodomises the envious son, or what have you. This argument of principle could then be tailored to the particular features of Ruskin's predicament, and some explanation offered of why the snake-as-penis, in some of his dreams at least, had women's breasts, why it was the small leech-like serpent that clung to his neck, and so on.

Without wishing to diminish the force of such arguments, down-to-earth or psychoanalytic, it is nonetheless tempting to go back to snakes and start again. For although Ruskin's snake dreams were ones of horror, others dream of snakes in a spirit of discovery and illumination. More or less simultaneously with the first serious onslaught of snake dreams upon Ruskin's sanity, the German chemist Kekulé was wrestling with a problem of a purely technical nature: the structure of benzene. The molecular formula of benzene had been established in 1834 as consisting of six carbon atoms and six hydrogen atoms. It was also clear that its structure must be one in which all six hydrogen atoms occupied positions that were equivalent. Baffled, Kekulé fell asleep and dreamt:

'Again the atoms were juggling before my eyes . . . my mind's eye, sharpened by repeated sights of a similar kind, could now distinguish larger structures of different forms and in long chains, many of them close together; everything was moving in a snake-like and twisting manner. Suddenly, what was this? One of the snakes got hold of its own tail and the whole structure was mockingly twisting in front of my eyes. As if struck by lightning, I awoke. . . . Let us learn to dream, gentlemen, and then we may perhaps find the truth.'[8]

Kekulé awoke with the insight that benzene is structured as a ring; more specifically, that its six carbon atoms are arranged in a six-sided figure, in which pairs of carbon atoms are double-bonded. Such a structure explained many of the observable properties of benzene, and was accepted as definitive for a quite a while.[9] The shortcomings of his model notwithstanding, Kekulé's achievement stands.

127

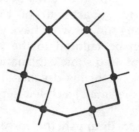

This cyclohexatriene structure is expressed in modern textbooks in the form:

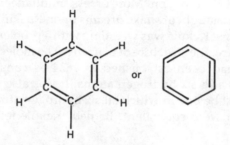

Like millions of others before and since, the chemist Kekulé dreamt of snakes, in his case the snakes of classical legend that swallow their own tails; but for him this ancient symbol performed the invaluable service of solving – or partially solving – a scientific problem.[10]

The idea of the snake or snake-like is obviously part of our currency. It comes easily to mind and can serve a variety of purposes: on the one hand, it can act as a focus for sexual guilt or disgust; on the other, it can produce the answer to a riddle in physical science. Is there any rationale for the recurrence of such images? Although hard evidence is lacking, a circumstantial case of sorts can be made. It is little more than a metaphor, but it is worth rehearsing, nonetheless.

At its heart is the idea that the human mind is genetically endowed with a repertoire of routes, patterns, pathways or trajectories. These, it is assumed, establish themselves in a variety of ways. Some are of current adaptive significance. Others will once have had an adaptive significance which they have since lost, and which linger on as 'atavisms'. Yet more will have evolved 'selfishly' and, to date, have no adaptive significance at all. All express themselves in practice not as specific ideas or skills, but as ideas and skills that each individual representative of the species finds it easy or natural to acquire and use. As a species, for instance, we inherit the ability to use language in a way that dogs do not. It is a skill that comes easily, and is in that respect part of our genetic specification.

There seems no reason why the snake, along with other recurrent images like that for example of the underground chamber, should not have a place within such a scheme as an atavism. An acute sensitivity to snake-like shapes could well have been of survival value to our remote ancestors; and it could now linger on as part of our mental furniture, available to each of us as a vehicle for trains of thought – Ruskin's sexual dilemma, Kekulé's musings about benzene – that have no bearing whatever on the adaptive purpose for which they were originally evolved.

The idea of the atavistic survival of genetically redundant information is now gaining currency among evolutionary biologists; the same may be said of the notion that genes may evolve selfishly, without regard to the organism's adaptive needs. Although the field is speculative, and experiments still risk being outnumbered by hypotheses, one of the studies cited in support of the atavism deserves a place in any book about dreams. It achieves a surreality of effect rarely approached by surreal art and never, in my experience, exceeded. It is that of the hen's teeth.

Although they once had them, it is sixty million years since birds displayed teeth. But their capacity to produce teeth, this experiment suggests, has survived. In the embryo, the development of teeth depends on the interaction of two sorts of embryonic issue; the inner and outer, or mesenchyme and epithelial. The inner can produce bone of its own accord; the outer of its own accord can produce enamel; but only through the interaction of inner and outer does a third substance, dentin, come about. In the millions of generations that separate the modern hen from its toothed forebears, the inner (but not the outer) tissue has lost its capacity to play an effective part in this interaction. As a result, hens are now toothless.

Two experimenters, Kollar and Fisher, demonstrated this by

combining outer tissues from the relevant part of five-day-old chick embryos with inner tissue from the embryos of mice, and leaving the tissues to grow together inside the eyes of adult nude mice. (Where else, as Stephen Gould asks, can one expect to find an open space, filled with fluid that does not circulate?) In some cases, there grew not only dentin but teeth; and in one instance a tooth that looked less like that of a mouse than that of an extinct bird.[11]

The debate about the redundancy of genetic information is a technical one.[12] Some DNA is redundant, it seems, in the sense that it has evolved 'selfishly', without ever having had an influence over the phenotype, the shape the body actually takes; some is redundant in the sense that it is atavistic, having once had an influence over the phenotype that it has since lost, hens' teeth being a case in point. Both sorts of redundancy, it seems, are compatible with fresh adaptations at the level of the phenotype. Indeed, without such redundancies, it has been suggested, species might lack the genetic resources which enable them to adapt to environmental pressures that are novel.

If the modern hen embodies atavisms in this way, human beings no doubt can too; and these could well encompass not only bodily structure and function, but instinctual patterns of behaviour and the thought processes linked to them. Atavisms that can be revealed by adjustments of embryonic tissue are one thing, of course; those that linger in the mind waiting to find a use are another altogether. They are so dissimilar, in fact, that the use of the same word to refer to them both amounts almost to a pun. It does seem, nevertheless, that the universalities of thought that so fascinated Jung may be re-entering the pale of legitimate scientific speculation.

Should they succeed in doing so, we will have the opportunity to rediscover, in passing, how formal Jung's beliefs about the inherited, archetypal, primordial aspects of human thought were. The concept of the archetype, Jung observes, 'is derived from the repeated observation that, for instance, the myths and fairy tales of world literature contain definite motifs which crop up everywhere'. These images he calls archetypal ideas, and sees them as deriving from a more fundamental pattern, the archetype itself.

'Again and again I encounter the mistaken notion that an archetype is determined in regard to its content, in other words, that it is a kind of unconscious idea (if such an expression be admissible). It is necessary to point out once more that archetypes are not determined as regards their content, but only as regards their form and then only to a very limited degree.'

A specific archetypal idea has its content determined when it becomes conscious and is 'filled out with the material of conscious experience'. Its form, however, Jung compares to 'the axial system of a crystal'. In itself, it is 'empty and purely formal, nothing but a *facultas praeformandi*, a possibility of representation which is given *a priori*'.[13]

There is little here to frighten even the most squeamish. Read at all sympathetically, Jung's views seem at times positively glacial in their commitment to formality – after decades of atomism in psychology, a refreshing tendency. (If everyone stares at the trees, there is no one to notice the design of the park in which both trees and observers stand.) It may prove that Ruskin's snakes and Kekulé's can be explained more parsimoniously as precipitates within sophisticated sensibilities of a shared Protestant culture. Even so, the notion of ancient residues and atavisms – of the snake-like as part of the mind's furniture awaiting a use – seems by no means an outrageous one.

Notes

(1) Rosenberg (1963), p. 168. His *The Darkening Glass* is a wonderfully vivid evocation of Ruskin's psychic state.
(2) Ibid., p. 190.
(3) Ibid., p. 191.
(4) Ibid., p. 213.
(5) Storr (1983) provides a valuable introduction to Jung's theorising, and helps the sceptic to see why Jung, like Isaac Newton, was so fascinated by apparently recondite topics like alchemy.
(6) These decision trees are set out more fully in Chapter 3 of my

Bodies of Knowledge (1982). References to the relevant literatures on sex and gender will be found there.

(7) Jung (1964), p. 67.

(8) Brook (1983), p. 139.

(9) More recently, Kekulé's model has been found lacking in certain respects; for instance, it predicts that bond lengths will be unequal, whereas the evidence of X-ray diffraction shows all the bonds between carbon atoms to be of equal length. This and other difficulties have, for the time being, been resolved to the satisfaction of most chemists by postulating a model in which the hexagon is regular, and in which hydrogen atoms execute butterfly-shaped orbits, thus creating rings of charge both above and below the plane of the molecule, yielding a pattern somewhat like a beefburger:

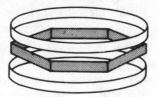

(10) Another story in the same vein concerns the discoverer of the sewing machine. The natural place for the eye of a needle, historical precedent establishes, is at its top. Elias Howe could find no way of building such a needle into a machine that would sew. He then dreamt of savages who demanded that he invent a sewing-machine within twenty-four hours. He failed and was sentenced to death – by spears that had eye-shaped holes in their tips. He awoke with the knowledge he needed: that of needles with eyes in their tips not in their tops: Cohen (1979), p. 262.

(11) Gould (1983), pp. 177–86.

(12) See, e.g., Gould and Lewontin (1979), Orgel and Crick (1980), Doolittle and Sapienza (1980). Gould's (1983) essays are of exemplary clarity, and provide the outsider with access to a field in which he would otherwise lack bearings.

(13) Storr (1983), p. 415.

CHAPTER TEN

Individuals Differ

The principle of the waking context need not be oppressively restricting; and in many ways Freud's dream about Irma, discussed in Chapter 8, remains the ideal example. It operates so transparently on two levels at once. It is a response – a revealing if not very attractive one – to his waking preoccupation with Fliess's bungled operation on Emma's nose. It is also a signal, as in Ruskin's case, of a deeper transition in the internal economy of his life: the step that was to lead him from neurology to psychoanalysis.

Within the discussion of residues, there lurks a further principle, however – in this text, the third of three. It is obvious, but has implications that are usually overlooked. It lies in the individual differences we each display. We differ in how we think while awake. We differ in how we think while asleep. And we differ in how we manage the traffic between one realm of thought and another.

The casual assumption in laboratory research is often that such differences are noise in the system, and do not much matter. The usual assumption in the psychoanalytic world, in contrast, is that they do matter, but that there nonetheless exists a satisfactory pattern, towards which everyone should ideally be encouraged to gravitate. The claim in this chapter and the next is that while individual differences do matter a great deal, no ideal pattern exists. On the contrary, there is rich variety, and it is highly desirable that this should be so. Patterns of sleep and dreaming, the recall of dreams, waking intelligence, patterns of personality, ways of life and differences in culture, far from being randomly related, all lock together into patterns. From the existence of these patterns, two possibilities flow. The first is that differences in 'fit' between sleeping and waking thought may constitute telling evidence of our adaptive powers. The second is that those who engage in polemic about the dream, whether attacking it as rubbish or exalting it as the source of all inspiration, may well be composing their own autobiographies out loud. Dream theorising, in other words, may prove to be a prime venue for the deployment of personal prejudices in academic guise. The purpose of this chapter is to root these possibilities in experimental evidence: to show how individual differences in sleep and dreaming are linked to significant features of our waking lives.

As has already been established, processes of thought can follow two quite different routes: they can converge onto a solution, or they can diverge from a point of origin in a variety of directions which is in principle unlimited:

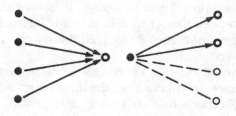

This difference can easily be operationalised in terms of mental measurements: on the one hand, the typical item in an IQ test; on the other, open-ended tests that invite the individual to think, for example, of as many uses as he can for a brick or a paper-clip.

Faced with such tasks, individuals differ. Within a roomful of university students, all of whom are intelligent in the colloquial sense, these differences can take extreme forms. The student whose IQ score places him in the top half of one per cent in the nation as a whole, can stare into space, baffled, and produce only one or two commonplace uses for a paperclip. In contrast, his neighbour, whose IQ score may be only a few points above the national average, can think of uses that are as clever as they are diverse: some witty, some ingenious, some far-fetched. The first kind of person is referred to as a 'converger': the second as a 'diverger'. There are in addition, of course, the 'all-rounders' who are equally good or bad at both IQ tests and open-ended tests.

Convergers and divergers were at first thought to differ in terms of their creativeness: Getzels and Jackson, who pioneered this kind of research in America, referred to the convergers as High IQs and to divergers as High Creatives. It soon became clear, though, that this difference was heavily overlaid with cultural considerations: convergers showed a strong tendency to be physical scientists, divergers to be specialists in arts subjects like English literature and history.[1]

More slowly, it became apparent that these differences were ones that implicated the personality, in that each individual's response was influenced by his habits of internal control. And far from being a question of repression, as old-fashioned psycho-analytic theories had led one to expect, these controls were so subtle as at times to elude description. They turned on such distinctions as that between what is acknowledged and unacknowledged, and on notions like those of personal identity and accountability. It was found, for instance, that the fluency with which convergers produced uses for objects improved out of all recognition if they were given clear instructions and examples. In effect, their response was to say 'So *that's* what you want. Why didn't you say so in the first place?'[2]

On one occasion, I invited a roomful of intelligent young men whom I had already tested some months before to answer the uses-of-objects test again: first, as if they were Robert Higgins, a successful computer engineer, and then as John McMice, the well-known artist, a man who is uninhibited and bohemian, and who likes to shock people with coarse or gruesome jokes. As Higgins, their responses were predictably constrained. As McMice, some were willing to pour onto the page outrageous and disgusting reveries – and this on the slenderest of excuses, because they had put their own names on their answer sheets and were readily identifiable.

One fifteen-year-old mathematician, answering as himself, had been willing to offer only generalised and unspecific violence:

SHOE: use shoe to knock out and laces to strangle. . . .
SUITCASE: suffocate animals.

But as John McMice, he was altogether more forthcoming:

MILK BOTTLE: Masturbate with it. Cut my mother's neck

with a broken bit. Would have an interesting effect if broken up and shot in little bits at a nude. The milk would be good to drown someone in. Pump it up someone's nose, vagina. Could make a pattern of interesting scars on a little boy's arse. . . .
CAR TYRE: Run over someone with it and squash their intestines, genitals, faces. Watch it slimily crush them. Then the car would skid. Fill it with lead, coat with steel, attach with chain to man's penis.

Forcefully, one is reminded of Jung's aphorism: 'It is on the whole probable that we continually dream, but that consciousness makes such a noise that we do not hear it.'[3] What is at issue, it seems, is the maintenance of a public role or persona. Those aspects of our recollected dreams or fantasies that do not fit a particular public performance are shelved. It is not that they are repressed; simply that they are left unacknowledged – they are not voiced.

One would clearly predict, on the strength of such studies, that if markedly convergent and markedly divergent individuals were invited to spend the night in a sleep laboratory and were woken when they showed every physiological sign of dreaming, they would differ sharply in what they recalled. The convergers should recall only a proportion of their dreams, whereas divergers should recall nearly all of them. And that is just what one finds. Mark Austin, a research student of mine in Edinburgh, did this experiment and found that whereas divergers almost always recalled a dream when woken in the midst of REM sleep, convergers do so on only fifty per cent of occasions. Either they said that they were dreaming but could not remember what the dream was about or they said that they had not been dreaming at all.[4]

In a second phase of these Edinburgh dream-recall experiments, Michael Holmes introduced an important refinement. He realised that a finding reported in the United States by Molinari and Foulkes had a special bearing on the case.[5] Their evidence indicated that REM sleep is more complex than it seems. The curious flickerings of the eyes that give the REM phase its name had previously been treated as more or less continuous. Molinari and Foulkes noted, though, that these flickerings were intermittent, bouts of rapid movement being interspersed with periods in which the eyes were more or less still. They awoke individuals from both sorts of sleep: when their eyes were flickering and also when their eyes were not. The result was striking. If their eyes were flickering when they were awoken, sleepers recalled dreams that were in Freud's sense 'primary': apparently uncoordinated eruptions into consciousness of images that seemed bizarre. If their eyes were still, on the other hand, the dreams recalled were 'thought-like': while asleep, the individuals in question seem to have been telling themselves stories or quietly musing, much as they might when awake.[6]

Holmes's research confirmed this distinction, and he gives examples in his thesis which make the differences between the 'dream-like' and 'thought-like' dream plain.[7] The first transcript is of a primary dream, and it reads, as primary dreams so often do, like the rudiments of a poem. It unsettled the student who reported it, and afterwards he took an unusually long time to get back to sleep:

Can you tell me the very last thing that was passing through your mind just before I woke you?
'It's a bit mixed up. . . . I seemed to be playing conkers . . . with this girl. She was playing with . . . a diamond I think, big and flashing. I had an ordinary conker, and every time she hit my conker it . . . hurt me for some reason. . . .'
Go on.
'I'm not sure how I came to be doing this . . . earlier I . . . can't remember.'
What was the very last thing?
'. . . My conker had just been hit . . . and I had this . . . it was more a flash in front of my eyes. . . . I found it uncomfortable. I can't explain this one well, it's all jumbled up.'
Was there visual imagery?
'Yes.'

The next transcript is of a thought-like or 'secondary' dream:

Can you tell me the very last thing that was passing through your mind just before I woke you?
'Yes, just a minute. . . . I was relating a story of having beer tipped over my head. . . . The actual beer-tipping operation

hadn't happened in the dream or whatever, but I was relating the story to a friend, called John, about being in a bar and having beer tipped over my head.'
Anything else?
'No, just sitting at a table. . . . On my left-hand side was a girl called Val and John was sitting opposite me and that was all.'
Was there visual imagery?
'Yes, his face was quite plain. . . . John was sort of casting his eyes to heaven and laughing.'
So what was the very last thing passing through your mind?
'I was just saying they had picked up the frame and tipped it over my head and it was full of beer. The frame, I explained, was the thing they drank out of, they didn't drink out of mugs or glasses or anything. It was a wooden frame.'

There are also dreams, within the thought-like or secondary category, that are more purely a matter of musing:

Can you tell me the very last thing that was passing through your mind just before I woke you?
'. . . I was thinking about blood sports. . . .'
Anything else?
'No. . . . I was just thinking about it. . . . The very last thing I was thinking about was Jimmy Edwards for some reason and he's in favour of it and I was just trying to think of someone who is not.'
Was there visual imagery?
'No, none at all.'

This evidence suggests that the sleeper is 'dreaming' when his eyes are flickering in the REM phase, 'thinking' when they are not. In turn, these 'thought-like' dreams are strongly reminiscent of those reported from other parts of the sleep cycle. Unfortunately, the natural history of this relationship between stages in the sleep cycle and dream experience is still somewhat scrappy, but it does seem that, contrary to the impression created over the last twenty-five years or so, dreams of one kind or another occur all through the night; that almost all of them are forgotten the next morning; and that they take on a special quality during the rapid-eye-movement phase. It is then that we experience the sort of dream that Foulkes and his collaborator describe as an eruption from the unconscious and as an intrusion which is ego-alien.[8]

The most obviously remarkable feature of Holmes's results was his discovery that while divergers' recall remained consistently good under both conditions, his convergers showed a sharp improvement: rather weak at recalling their dream-like dreams, they were excellent at recalling their thought-like ones.

In addition, he found that his convergers and divergers differed in the pattern that their REM sleep took. The total amount of rapid eye movement displayed by convergers and divergers in the course of the night was, on average, very nearly the same. It was differently distributed, however. Convergers, he found, tended to sleep less than divergers; to go into REM sleep for the first time earlier in the night; to concentrate their REM sleep, relatively speaking, into the earlier part of the night; and to spend less of their REM sleep with their eyes still.[9] It is as if convergers need their REM sleep – and their dreams – more urgently than do divergers; and that they work this need through more expeditiously. Yet it is the converger, not the diverger, who is the more likely to forget the thoughts that his dream sleep contains.

The implication is that, during the relatively lengthy periods that he spends in REM sleep but with his eyes still, the diverger is doing his best to make sense of the bizarre imagery that he has just experienced during the preceding bout of eye movement. The diverger it seems, accommodates the apparently irrational aspects of his experience, musing on it, weaving it by one means or another into a story or argument. He assimilates, intellectualises, rationalises. The converger tends, in contrast, to segregate his irrational imagery; to block it at the natural boundary between sleeping and waking thought.[10] The costs and benefits of these two strategies are the obvious ones. The diverger has access to a resource of potential value; but when the time comes for disciplined and impersonal argument, he will be subject to internally generated distractions. The converger finds it natural to clear the decks for ratiocination, but does so at the cost of detaching himself from the intuitive insights that he is bound from time to time to need. The diverger's strategy predisposes him towards those sort of waking activity in which the personal and intuitive are dominant; the converger's suits him to those in

139

which intuitive insights are either irrelevant or can be borrowed from someone else when the need arises.

Thus far, both converger and diverger are seen as performing consistently. The way in which they manage the traffic between the intuitive and rational aspects of their thought remains substantially the same, whether they are awake or asleep at the time: the one segregating, the other assimilating. A principle of compensation is at work too, though. The converger, massively committed to order and rationality while awake, has an unusually urgent need to dream. The diverger, whose commitment to rationality and order while awake is less pronounced, dreams less urgently. Convergers dream at least as floridly, it seems, as do divergers, but as soon as they cross the threshold from sleep to waking they have ready access only to those of their dreams that resemble the thinking they do while they are awake. The greater the commitment to common sense and rationality while awake, in other words, the more important the boundary between the waking and sleeping thought becomes.

A half-hidden moral of Holmes's results is that the recollection of primary (but not secondary) dreams may after all be disruptive to the orderly execution of waking skills. The more committed an individual is to a culture that demands of him the fluently impersonal deployment of knowledge and techniques – the more deeply immersed he is, for example, in the worlds of technology or physical science – the more disruptive the recall of primary material could well become.

A third Edinburgh dream-recall study spells out this implication, and also refines it in two important respects. Margaret Cormack and Peter Sheldrake asked biology students, convergent and divergent, male and female, to keep dream diaries.[11] They found a marked sex difference. Among the males, divergers recalled dreams nearly five times as often as convergers, just as Austin's and Holmes's evidence led them to expect. But among the young women, the equivalent difference was relatively slight. The odd ones out, in other words, were the male convergers. This sex difference is intriguing because it relates so conspicuously to others: notably, the tendency of males to dominate those forms of intellectual life – physical science, engineering – which require the subjugation of the intuitive in the interests of impersonal cerebration. It may well be that gifted young women tend to fight shy of these disciplines precisely because this segregation is one that does not come as easily to them as it does to some young men.

There is a hint in Cormack and Sheldrake's data about how such sex differences might arise. They found a surprisingly strong connection between the amount of convergence or divergence each female student displayed and the point she had reached in her menstrual cycle. Those tested in the week before ovulation showed a tendency to be classified as 'divergers', while those tested in the fortnight after ovulation tended to emerge as 'convergers'. After the event this finding makes sense because the Uses-of-Objects test is demonstrably sensitive to attitude and mood.[12] It seems, in other words, that a woman's position on the convergence/divergence dimension could prove to vary quite markedly in the course of each month. These changes in turn could be sufficient to disturb the sustained 'instrumentality' of attitude and self-perception that a career in physical science or technology seems at the moment to demand.

Cormack and Sheldrake also found that, at the outset, convergers were more reluctant than divergers to take part in a dream-diary study. This, one would have predicted. Once the study was under way, though, it was the divergers who were the more likely to fall by the wayside. Among the men, convergers kept their dream diaries on average for nearly twice as long as the divergers; divergers were nearly four times as likely to miss days here and there; and it was two convergers – not two divergers – who, at the end of the twelve-week span, volunteered for a further stint.

These differences could perhaps be explained away in terms of the convergers' greater dutifulness. One diverger's reasons for giving up suggest a more searching explanation though:

'I'm afraid that I'm going to admit defeat. To start with, it was great fun remembering my dreams, but now I'm beginning to feel quite a strain in it. It's difficult to put. It's almost as if I was looking at an emotional release, which because I try to remember it is no longer released. It seemed that before I began this experiment the dreams I remembered were enjoyable and now they frighten me.'

Dream recall, we tend to assume, is good for us; a knitting together of threads. Taken together, the Edinburgh studies suggest on the contrary that there exists a systematically related pattern of pros and cons associated with permeability to the non-rational; and that individuals differ not so much in being more 'mature' or 'healthy' than one another, but in the path they find it natural to follow, and in the risks, given that path, that they then find it possible to take.

Although they do not advance our knowledge of sleep and dream recall in any definitive way, these Edinburgh studies do help establish a frame of reference, and it is this, at the moment, that we most urgently need.

At the centre of this framework is a natural boundary: that between sleeping and the waking thought. Linked to it are a number of apparently separate facets of each individual's life: his pattern of sleep, the character of his dreams, his ability to recall those dreams on waking, the bias of his waking intelligence, the disposition of his personality, the way of life he fashions for himself, the academic career he follows, and the adult culture into which this career leads him. There exists a great deal of evidence to show, for example, that patterns of marriage, fertility and divorce vary from one academic speciality to another: arts specialists from scientists, biological scientists from physical scientists, chemists from physicists, and so on. Eminent British physicists, for instance, reveal rates of divorce six times as high as those of eminent British chemists.[13]

At the level of ascertainable fact, these patterns are loose-knit – questions of moderate correlation rather than of tight one-to-one linkage. But they gain strength and coherence by being embedded within systems of stereotypical belief that are highly consistent internally, and that are engrained in our minds from a remarkably early age. We know that the stereotype of the typical scientist is already established in its fully fledged form in the minds of intelligent young eleven year olds, before they have had any exposure to specialised science teaching. Also, that in the course of secondary education, during which a good deal of science is taught, this stereotype alters very little. We know too that among seventeen year olds these stereotypical beliefs are shared more or less equally by those who reject science as a career and those who are already committed to it: the typical scientist is seen as intelligent, manly and dependable, but also as unimaginative, hard and cold, by young scientists and young non-scientists alike.[14]

The existence of such patterns, a complex mixture of fact and fantasy, does not determine which path a given individual will follow. Instead, it determines which paths he will perceive as natural or comfortable. The highly convergent young man who fails to recall his primary dreams is not excluded from the arts; and if he enters them, he could well find there a niche that suits his gifts. The likelihood is, though, that he will feel subtly out of his element – marginal. Likewise, the diverger whose access to his primary dreams is excellent is not excluded from science or technology, but the cast of his mind, the grain of his appetites and curiosities, will make him feel more at home elsewhere.[15]

The appropriate response to such regularities is not to rail against them, still less to launch a polemic from one vantage point against all others, but to look with care at the 'fit' between individual and niche. What *is* life like, say, for the diverger who becomes an engineer? Does he have that feeling, described by the novelist Kurt Vonnegut, of being 'somehow slightly off-balance all the time'.[16] Does he find, nonetheless, that he can complement the efforts of his more convergent colleagues from time to time in unexpected ways – and thus establish a role for himself as an 'ideas man'? And what, one wonders, is the effect of a niche that is psychologically alien upon his access to his own dreams? Do these remain florid, but become increasingly remote from his daily work – like those of the engineer in Chapter 8, who dreamt so vividly about works of art? Or do they gradually lose their vigour and emotional charge, and become more spectral?

To examine the relationship of the individual to his niche is to discover that bodies of knowledge seem incapable of growing without at the same time generating powerfully coercive orthodoxies. It is also to learn that radical advances are often made by outsiders: the men or women who are in some sense or other marginal to the discipline in question.[17] Thus originality may in practice prove to depend not just on access to one's intuitions, fantasies and dreams, nor even on being marginal to one's discipline – on being a physicist working among biologists, say, a woman working among men, a person from a regional background among cosmopolitans – but on expressions of

143

marginality that are more hidden and personal. It may spring from the need to cut across the grain of one's discipline, whatever it happens to be. Casting back, for example, to Cormack and Sheldrake's findings about female students and their menstrual cycles, it could be that women are potentially at their most creative in science in the week before ovulation, when they are at their most divergent; but at their most creative in the arts in the two weeks after ovulation, when they are in comparison convergent. On this argument, one is potentially creative when driven, for whatever reason, to adopt a line of thought that is incongruous, discrepant.

The critic, hostile to all mention of the dream in serious contexts, may be tempted to insist that the requirements of creative work, though dependent on marginality, can be met without reference to the dream: that we would be adequately equipped if we had no access to our sleeping thought at all. The evidence of this chapter suggests that an answer to him can be framed. But before saying what shape it takes, one must look with more care at the process of recall itself, and the steps whereby dreams are turned into words.

Notes

(1) Getzels and Jackson (1962); Hudson (1966), (1968).

(2) Hudson (1968). What is stable in an individual's personality is not his 'output', but the needs, fears and identifications on which that output depends. These are subject to local or more lasting realignment. A man may reveal one side of his nature when sober, another when drunk; one when at home, another when at work. His character may also alter, as many are said to, in mid-life. But even in such semi-permanent readjustments, the same elements, arguably, could be shuffled together into different configurations. Personal change, whether local or more enduring, is compatible, in other words, with the view that the elements of each individual's personality are for all practical purposes given, being determined by genetics, or the early environment, or the interaction of the one with the other.

(3) Quoted by Rycroft (1979), p. 32.

(4) Austin (1971). Austin, like Holmes, based his work on samples of males. Cohen (1979) mentions a number of studies carried out with American students that support Austin's findings. By now, divergence, specialisation in the arts or social sciences, and a 'creative' turn of mind are all linked quite firmly to good recall of primary dreams.

(5) Holmes (1973), (1976); Molinari and Foulkes (1969).

(6) Something went wrong, partially at least, when attempts were made to replicate this finding: see, e.g., Foulkes and Pope (1973). Cohen (1979) concludes that the original result must have been artefactual. On the other hand, Holmes's data echo those of the original study quite closely; and there is abundant evidence, in any case, of secondary or 'thinking' dreaming in other phases of the sleep cycle: Foulkes (1978), p. 90; Oswald (1980), p. 69. Such muddles – 'twice you see it, thrice you don't' – seem endemic in experimental psychology. In some cases, the effects are real, but are intermittently obscured by the influence of variables as yet unidentified. In others, they are the product of sampling errors, or of the experimenter's imagination.

(7) Holmes (1976), p. 99.

(8) Foulkes (1978), p. 90; Oswald (1980), p. 71. Obvious instances of primary dreaming in non-REM sleep are the night terror; and also the images experienced in falling asleep and waking up. Foulkes concludes a little ruefully that while modern sleep-laboratory techniques have teased us with the possibility that dream states can be 'read from outside', this ability still eludes us: Foulkes (1978), p. 356. Certainly, his own view of the differences between REM and non-REM dreaming is a complex one.

(9) The first REM period lasted on average thirteen minutes for Holmes's convergers, only eight minutes for his divergers; whereas the fourth REM period lasted twenty-eight minutes for convergers, and thirty-nine minutes for divergers. Moreover, his convergers were only half as likely as his divergers to display 'quiescence' – that is to say, a page of polygraph recording lasting twenty seconds without eye movement: Holmes (1976). As Crick has pointed out (personal communication, 19 December 1984), these physio-logical differences between convergers and divergers could

be genetic in origin – akin, for example, to that between people born right- and left-handed – and could reflect the efficiency with which the two sorts of individual clear their neural nets of parasitic information. If he is right, differences in character could stem from relatively simple differences in cerebral organisation.

(10) The idea that episodes of 'secondary cognitive elaboration' are functionally related to the 'primary visual experience' that immediately precedes them – that both are part of the same dream sequence – is one that Foulkes (1978) takes seriously, but it remains unproven. It could be that although the two sorts of thought follow one another they are largely or completely unrelated.

(11) Cormack and Sheldrake (1974).

(12) Hudson (1968). From the vantage point of the traditional mental-measurements man, this feature of open-ended tests renders them 'unreliable' and therefore useless. In the hands of the less blinkered, this property makes them all the more revealing.

(13) Hudson and Jacot (1971), Hudson, Johnston and Jacot (1972), Hudson, Jacot and Sheldrake (1973), Hudson (1973).

(14) Hudson (1967), (1968). The image of the typical artist takes shape only gradually, though, in the course of adolescence. It is as if these stereotypical beliefs about science and the arts were caricatures and precipitates of the crises of latency and adolescence respectively: Hudson (1975).

(15) Kuhn (1963) has argued that the diverger is of special relevance to science when the field in question enters a 'revolutionary' phase. Compatible with this view is the discovery of exceptionally high rates of divorce among scientists who rise to eminence during turbulent phases in their disciplines' growth: Hudson and Jacot (1971).

(16) Vonnegut (1982), p. 74.

(17) Hudson and Jacot (1985). Of special interest is the evidence that scientists of Jewish background are massively more likely to reach the highest flights in their own disciplines than those whose background is Catholic: Zuckerman (1977). There are, in other words, outsiders and outsiders.

CHAPTER ELEVEN

From Dreams into Words

It is not easy to make sense of the Edinburgh sleep and dream-recall studies amidst the conceptual baggage left behind by previous generations of theory-builders: the emphasis, still hard to escape, on the clumsy and often irrelevant distinction between conscious and unconscious, and the insistence on crudely forthright mechanisms of control – repression, for example, and the censor. More helpful are distinctions like that between the avowed and unavowed, the acknowledged and unacknow-ledged, and mechanisms that are more subtly efficacious, like the individual's sense of his own identity, or the extent to which he sees himself as accountable for what is said or done.

At the heart of the Edinburgh studies and of any attempt to examine the place of the dream in waking life is the process of recall: the steps whereby one calls up and entertains mental events now past, and translates them into sentences that are acceptably intelligible both to an audience and to oneself. Like the souls of the dead in Virgil's *Aeneid*, dreams stand with 'their hands outstretched in yearning for the other shore'. The ques-tion, practically speaking, is how they are to be ferried across.

The correct context for such an examination is the study of memory. Unfortunately, there is an established tradition of experimental research on memory which leads one towards the view that recall is, in essence, a matter of accuracy. Good recall is accurate and comprehensive recall; and, for the rest, one is dealing with failures and distortions – information that is lost or scrambled. A slightly less unsophisticated view treats recall as at heart a question of translation: a movement from the non-discursive to the discursive mode – from ideas as they exist inside the head to the sentences that come out of people's mouths. But neither formulation begins to do justice to the phenomena of remembering and describing. The aim of this chapter, therefore, is to create a context for the future discussion of dream recall that is more realistic. It does so by looking at a handful of literary examples of recollection; by drawing some rudimentary diagrams of boundaries and events surrounding them; and by treating one boundary in particular as a metaphor for the boundary that separates sleeping from waking thought – the one, namely, that separates the world in which a film is manufactured from the world of the spectator who watches it and then attempts to say what he has seen.

Literature has many lessons for the psychologist, most of them blithely ignored. Among the most compelling are those that deal with the relation of past to present and the extent to which past events invade present ones. People and places, apparently trivial, are heavily freighted in recollection with unspoken significance. Others that, on common-sense grounds, ought to have one set of meanings attached to them carry quite different meanings. And yet others that ought, on the same common-sensical grounds, to be pregnant with significance have none at all. It is in the context of such apparently arbitrary migrations of meaning that the recall of the dream, a special sort of past, should properly be set.

T. S. Eliot is one of many to observe how, in waking life, emotion seems to gather, dream-like, around a handful of images from the past:

> 'Why, for all of us, out of all that we have heard, seen, felt, in a lifetime, do certain images recur, charged with emotion, rather than others? The song of one bird, the leap of one fish, at a particular place and time, the scent of one flower, an old woman on a German mountain path, six ruffians seen through an open window playing cards at night at a small French railway junction where there was a water-mill.'[1]

More recent events, too, though more fully recallable, often remain inexplicable in their influence, sometimes reassuring, sometimes obscurely menacing or disruptive: a party, an unexpected meeting, a fragment of a film or play. In *A Dance to the Music of Time*, a series of novels exemplary for the skill with which they anatomise the shifts of perception that occur as relationships between individuals evolve, Anthony Powell describes one such instance: a literary conference in post-war Venice. At this conference, there had been a great deal of gossip and some scandal, but none of this had seemed to touch at all closely the narrator himself. On returning to London, 'established priorities, personal continuities, the confused scheme of things making up everyday life' are re-established, yet the recollection of Venice lingers uneasily:

'The Conference settled down in the mind as a kind of dream, one of those dreams laden with the stuff of real life, stopping just the right side of nightmare, yet leaving disturbing under-currents to haunt the daytime, clogging sources of imagination – whatever those may be – causing their enigmatic flow to ooze more sluggishly than ever, periodically cease entirely.'[2]

Even more tellingly dream-like are those people and places that ought in recollection to be fraught with complex emotion, but are devoid of it – or that have a potency of meaning that switches on and off unpredictably, like a poorly wired light bulb. Powell catches some of these adroitly too. In another novel from the same series, the narrator comes face to face, quite unexpectedly, with a former mistress, now married to the military attaché of a foreign power:

' "You must come and see us", she said. "We're really not properly moved in yet. I expect you know we've only just arrived. The appointment was quite a surprise – due to a change of Government." She mentioned an address in Knightsbridge, as it happened not far from the flat at the back of Rutland Gate, where once, quite naked, she had opened the door when we were lovers. Like so many things that have actually taken place, the incident was now wholly unbeliev-able. How could this chic South American lady have shared with me embraces, passionate and polymorphous as those depicted on the tapestry of Luxuria that we had discussed together when we had met at Stourwater? Had she really used those words, those very unexpected expressions, she was accustomed to cry out aloud at the moment of achievement? Once I had thought life unthinkable without her. How could that have been, when she was now only just short of a perfect stranger?'[3]

The point of these examples is not that these recollections of waking thought are dream-like and therefore exceptional. On the contrary: it is that they are dream-like and normal – so normal that, in practice, we scarcely notice how dream-like they are. The intuitive and more orderly exist on both sides of the boundary that separates sleeping from waking thought. The essential difference between the two, if there is one, is that in our waking lives we have tasks, task-masters and an immediate audience to satisfy whereas, when asleep, we do not. Awake, we are harnessed; asleep we are unharnessed. And, one suspects, the longer our waking lives are free from tasks, task-masters and an audience, the more our sleeping and waking thoughts will tend to resemble one another, and the less conspicuous the boundary between them will seem. But conspicuous or not, the boundary is there, a fact of life, and across it flows traffic in either direction; waking thought becomes the raw material for dreams, and dreams in their turn are often recalled, sometimes described, and occasionally understood.

Formal questions are at issue as well as factual ones.[4] A boundary is a boundary in the first place in as much as it segregates. And, characteristically but by no means invariably, it segregates by means of its influence on a traffic that passes across it: the frontier post that filters immigrants and emigrants by means of passports and visas; a membrane that regulates the chemical exchange between organism and environment; the river Styx, 'flood of deadly hate', that separates living from dead. The traffic may be free, blocked or in some way modified, restricted or translated; it may be one-way or two-way; and it may be symmetrical or asymmetric:

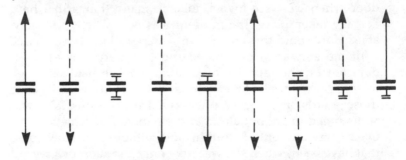

If solid arrows are allowed to stand for free traffic, dotted ones for traffic that is restricted or modified, and the cross-hatching sign for traffic that is blocked, we already have nine options.

The boundary can be set out as a circle, it being sleeping thought that is enclosed. If this is done, a variety of configurations result, some stable, others not:

Of these, the top one has a chance of achieving equilibrium; the other two do not. The middle configuration is, in effect, that of a 'black hole': meanings pass freely from the waking to the sleeping, but nothing comes out. The third configuration is the reverse. The outflowing traffic is freer than the inflowing, and hence the arrangement is one that will tend to empty itself.

Sometimes, bounded spaces like these develop not merely a

rich external shape, but complex internal designs. These features are conspicuous in architecture; in the groundplans, for example, of certain mediaeval and renaissance buildings – here, of a 13th-century fortress, Castel del Monte:

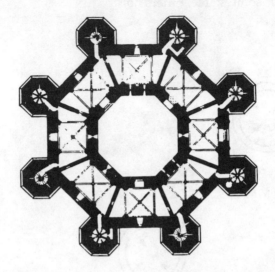

Of special interest in the present context is the possibility, displayed in the groundplan of Castel del Monte, that the figure will embody not merely one boundary but two, one within the other. If a second boundary is added, the inner can represent the threshold between sleeping and waking thought, and the outer the threshold between waking thought and the outside world:

This second boundary permits traffic like the first. The result is a rudimentary system. Again, some of its configurations are in principle stable, others not:

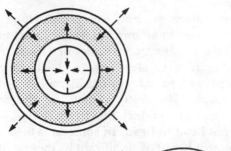

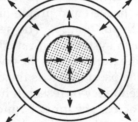

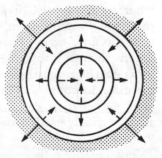

Each of these has a different tendency. That of the first is to concentrate meanings in the waking thought: a head packed with thoughts that can neither find adequate public expression nor be translated into dreams. The tendency of the second is centripetal, gathering meanings in sleeping thought: a state that might be seen as reminiscent of Rilke's before his extraordinary outpouring, a condition ripe for precisely the kind of catastrophic reversal he in fact experienced. The third is centrifugal; the system that projects everything that it can absorb – the one sometimes characterised in terms of the actor who can utter everything he thinks and imagines but who, when he ceases to speak, seems quite empty.

The purpose of such simple diagrams, however, is not to typify different sorts of people, still less to accommodate the kinds of experimental detail generated in laboratory studies like those of Austin and Holmes. Rather it is to alert one to the hidden implications that the concept of a boundary brings in tow. Two of these are unmistakably plain. The first is that the dream landscape, the world of meanings on which the dream draws, is unlikely to be the same from head to head. In some, it is bleak, these diagrams suggest, almost bereft of significant incidents. In others, it is so densely packed and jungle-like as to threaten all but the most wary with suffocation. The second implication is that changes within such systems can reverberate. A change in the conditions governing traffic across the one boundary could in time influence the traffic passing across the other boundary too.

As it happens, the tendency of research has been to dwell on the sleepwards traffic across the inner boundary in this system, and to neglect the traffic in the opposite direction – the processes whereby recollected dreams are assimilated to the habits and rhythms of waking thought. This neglect is regrettable because it is in the finer grain of dream recall and in the skills of turning dream images into sentences that some of the most exciting prospects for research on individual differences are to be found.[5] In order to cope with this finer grain, we need a model or metaphor that we can unpack, one detail at a time. Ideal, and already widely used in dream-research circles, is the metaphor of the cinema.[6]

As a metaphor, the cinema has deep attractions. It enables us to distinguish clearly between the film studio, the world of preparation and construction, and what happens in the spectator's mind once the film in its finished state has hit the screen – the screen itself constituting the boundary or interface between one world and the other. On this analogy, Freud's dream theory is seen as a director's theory; a question of scenarios, shooting scripts, and footage left on the cutting-room floor; so too for that matter are 'bottom-up' theories like Crick and Mitchison's.

If dreams are constructed like films, one can see at once how the finished 'film', the one that the dreamer sees on his own internal screen, can be the end-product of all manner of apparently unrelated skills and contrivances. In the production of a film, for instance, images and sound track, although flowing from the same script, are usually married together late in the day. If, by analogy, we wrench a sleeper awake in the midst of REM – in the midst, as it were, of his process of dream production – we might reasonably expect to find the components of the finished dream, verbal and visual, primary and secondary, in a state of mutual dislocation.

A theory like Freud's, especially when set out as a flow chart as it is in Chapter 3, can be seen as summarising the film studio's internal organisation, and specifying the sequence in which departments make their contributions to the final product. One can see, too, how that internal organisation could over time generate 'parasitic' elements: bureaucracy and restrictive working practices being the equivalent, within the world of film production, of parasitic information in a neural network.[7]

The metaphor of the cinema also enables us to ask questions about personal responsibility and accountability that might otherwise seem dangerously elusive. We can ask whether the film the spectator sees is someone else's or his own. Is he the director, anxiously watching his own rushes; or is he a private citizen watching films at home on his own television or video screen? (And if he is at home, how much say does he have in the selection of what he sees? Is his choice limited by his wife's preferences or inhibitions, or by the presence of teenaged children in the house? To what extent, in other words, is he really alone when he watches?)

What happens inside the spectator's head, once he has seen the film, is important, too; and, in a sense, it has epistemological priority. From the inquiring psychologist's point of view, the dreamer is his only witness; an audience of one. We gain access to the film itself by listening to what the dreamer says about what he saw. It is the processes of dream recall and assimilation that hold the key. If we concentrate upon what the spectator makes of what he sees, the complexity of events is at once apparent. In unpacking them, one needs all the powers of doubt and cold-eyed scrutiny that are supposed to be the experimental psychologist's stock-in-trade.

Take a dream like the one Holmes records: that of the diamond-conker. It contains, in its recorded form, scraps of narrative, at least one startlingly paradoxical visual image, and also the sensation of discomfort. And it left behind it a sense of disquiet. What are the chances that this dream found its way, complete and unabridged, into the words that the student in question uttered to Holmes, waiting at the other end of the sleep laboratory's intercom?

Assume, for the sake of argument, that the images on the dreamer's internal screen were as vivid as the description implies. In principle they could have been blurred, poorly focused; the sound could have been out of synch. But take it that, technically speaking, all was well.[8] Assume too, for a moment, that the film is one that the spectator remembers in full. One can now envisage several quite different paths that this vivid experience might take en route to becoming a set of sentences.

Following one of these, the dreamer leaves the cinema and describes the film to an acquaintance he meets in the street, and does so to the best of his ability. What he says is edited, even so. As he puts his recollection of the film into words, the conventions of story-telling begin to take over. He wants to hold his friend's attention, and to make sense. As a result, he tells a story in which certain links are provided that in the film itself were lacking, and in which a number of the film's more subtly inscrutable elements – certain perplexing ambiguities, for example – are glossed over. Later, he tells his girlfriend about the film too. This time, he is less concerned to tell a good story, and feels free to stumble. Without realising that he has done so, he still glosses over two important details: the identity of the girl with the diamond-conker, and the extent to which she caused him actual pain. For a second time he has edited, matching the account he gives to what he intuitively perceives as his audience's vulnerabilities and needs.

Now, let us follow the dream on a second path, quite unlike the first. The film, again, is clearly remembered, but when the opportunity to describe it arises, the dreamer brushes his recollection aside in a conventional phrase. And he does so in this case, not because he is embarrassed or upset by what he has seen, which he perfectly well might have been, but because he is lost for words. He has, within his command, none of the verbal skills with which to translate what he has seen into sentences. It is a trick he does not know how to perform.

Perhaps, though, it is after all his memory of the film that is blurred; he finds it difficult to describe because he has to some extent forgotten what it was. There are two separate sorts of reason why this might be so. The first is that he might have been inattentive or distracted: he may have sat with his eyes glued to the screen, but his head full of student-union politics; or he may have paid close attention to the film at the time, but allowed all recollection of it to be swamped by other considerations the moment he stepped out of the cinema door.

The second reason is that, far from being inattentive or distracted, he was deeply shocked by what he saw. He may have perceived plainly what was happening on the screen but then repressed all memory of it. Or the shock could have been more immediate in its effect: it could have disturbed his perception, leaving him with no clear impressions to remember. Speaking for a moment in systematic terms, it is often assumed that the effect of trauma on memory occurs on the output side of the memory store. There is no reason, though, why it should not exert an influence on the input side too, with the result that some traumatic images, rather than being clearly encoded and then blocked, are poorly encoded in the first place.

These alternative paths from the dream image towards the sentence are easier to grasp when set out in terms of a decision tree, in which, for the psychologist, each branch represents the consequence of an interpretative choice.

To those already sceptical, a decision tree of this size can make dream interpretation seem a hopeless venture. This is doubly mistaken, however. There is nothing in it that does not apply equally to feats of recall that, although problematic, are accepted every day as a matter of course – for example, in a court of law: the recollection of an accident, or of an unexpectedly turbulent meeting or a sudden row; more dramatically, the victim's recollection of a bank robbery or rape. After any vivid experience, whether waking or sleeping, the same questions arise. What did the witness actually see? Can he put his experiences successfully into words? Advertently or inadvertently, does he edit – either because he wants to sustain an impression vis-à-vis his audience, or because he is shocked or ashamed?[9]

Dream Recall: The Interpretative Options

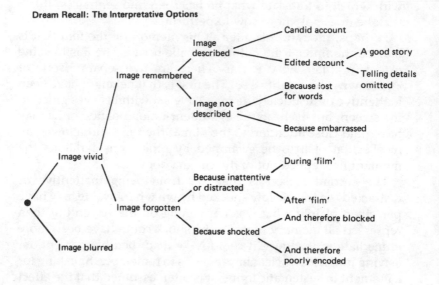

In any case, the paths that the decision tree describes are evidence of what immediately concerns us: the fact that individuals differ in the tactics and strategies they adopt in transferring meanings from one side of the boundary between sleeping and waking to the other. It is not only that convergers differ from divergers – there being routes in the tree that advertise themselves as convergent, others as divergent – but that they may also differ among themselves. There is more than one way of failing wholly to reveal what a dream was about; and more than one way, too, of giving an interlocutor an adequate impression of it. The decision tree enables one, in other words, to reach past the simple distinctions on which earlier research on convergers and divergers was based, towards differentiations between individuals that are more nearly rooted in what, when confronted with a baffling experience and the task of describing it, they actually do and say.

Notes

(1) Eliot (1953), p. 95.
(2) Powell (1974), p. 194.

(3) Powell (1971), p. 240.

(4) Catastrophe theory has a bearing on the boundary and its formal properties: see, e.g., Woodcock and Davis (1978).

(5) Puzzles remain on the sleeping side of the boundary, particularly the nature of the relationship between the dream's primary and secondary elements: Foulkes (1978). Pertinent perhaps is the item of sleep-laboratory lore which holds that the more gradually you allow someone in REM sleep to awaken, the more likely his dream report is to take a secondary, story-telling form.

(6) See, e.g., Hobson (1980).

(7) The metaphor of the parasite has already been quite widely used in systematic theorising within biology: see, e.g., Orgel and Crick (1980), Crick and Mitchison (1983). So far, this use has occmed impressionistic. Here, biologists might have something to learn from sociological research on the nature of bureaucracies.

(8) These quasi-mechanical aspects of the cinema analogy are by no means trivial. It is often assumed, for example, that the converger who is in REM sleep and whose eyes are flickering, yet who fails to recall a dream when awoken, has a dream that he forgets. There is no reason, though, why some obstacle should not from time to time intervene – either between projector and screen, or between screen and audience. There is no reason, in other words, why in some people conscious-ness of dream thought should not be intermittent or blocked.

(9) In detail, the interests of detective and psychologist diverge. The detective wants a full and accurate account; the psychologist is drawn to omissions and inaccuracies as interesting in their own right.

CHAPTER TWELVE

In Sum

The thesis of this book has been that dreams can be interpreted if they are approached in the same spirit that we approach poems, if we pay close attention to their waking context, and if we allow for the fact that individuals differ both in how they dream and how they assimilate what they have dreamt to their waking lives. Taken together, these three principles amount to a method; and within its bounds, dream interpretation could quite rapidly become 'scientific', in the sense that, like natural science, it is reasonably orderly and, in fits and starts, accumulative.

What of the dream's enemies, though? There are many sceptics who see the dream itself as marginal and any painstaking effort to discover its meaning as irrelevant to the needs of a society that is modern and changing. They might even be willing to use the dream's banishment as an index of the extent to which the society in question has evolved. Such a critic might well acknowledge the part that unconscious thought plays in creative endeavour, in the arts and sciences alike, but still deny that the dream itself has anything to contribute. As he might well point out, we could easily have evolved as a species which had access to its waking fantasies and reveries, and which dreamt, but which had no powers of dream recall. What would have been the loss? The answer, I think, comes in two parts: the first glib and probably wrong; the second more circumspect, and more awkward to state, but much more sweepingly radical in its implications.

The quick answer admits that while in all probability our science and technology would have developed quite satisfactorily, at the personal level we would be impoverished. Life would be like gardening, say, without a sense of smell. As poets, we would be predictable and lacklustre – and as lovers, perhaps, too. If, on the other hand, we had taken another evolutionary turning, and could all recall our dreams fluently, science and technology would have suffered. We would neither have

160

invented the internal combustion engine, nor discovered the petrol that makes it run. We would have more poetry than we now have, and more chaos – more, arguably, than we need of either. This is glib, however, in that it rests on assumptions about the relation of thought to action that are naive. A more cautious answer is far from easy to frame because, at present, we lack the necessary knowledge and sophistication. An attempt can be made, nonetheless.

This more cautious answer focuses on the imagination. We know that, as a species, we are able to act on the world imaginatively; to create what was not previously there and had not previously been thought of. What we do not know is how this happens, nor quite what influence on this process the dream is likely to exert. In edging towards an adequate account, three closely related arguments come into play: three prongs, as it were, of an argumentative fork.

The first prong concerns the mind's power to organise its own knowledge. It goes without saying that we must be responsive to external requirements, and must in some sense be driven by them. At the same time, we must have the power not only to anticipate and predict, but to generate new orders and sustain them, if necessary through long periods of apparent adversity. The importance of this capacity is perhaps obscured at the level of automata and of idealised neural networks, but is obvious at that of ordinary human exchange. In order to function satisfactorily, we must have the power to generate and sustain convictions, ideals and visions that prevent us from becoming socially tame, amenable to whatever regularities those in our immediate environment seek to impose upon us. The basic requirement in the design of any self-organising system is that it should have, built into it and continually sustained, the capacity not only to recognise and acknowledge patterns that are there, but to recognise and acknowledge patterns that, in the literal sense, are not. This is a function which the primary dream meets to a nicety.[1]

The second point concerns the risk that this power of self-organisation will be carried to excess. Our waking lives are in practice regulated by orthodoxies, platitudes, stories, prejudices and rules-of-thumb, all of which are inaccurate or inappropriate to greater or lesser degree. The dream earns its keep, within such

161

a system of meanings, not by offering better solutions, though this does happen from time to time, and on occasions memorably so, but by exerting a destabilising influence on habits of mind and patterns of thought that are rigid and wrong. On this second argument, in essence that of the surrealist in art, the dream is the mind's counter-attack on its own states of false consciousness and self-deception.[2]

3 / The third argument, and perhaps the most important, directs us towards areas of psychology as yet largely unexplored. Its point of departure is the fact that the apparatus of imaginative thought is compartmentalised. When theorising Freud often seemed to speak as if primary-process thought was homogeneous, a stew pot or cauldron; also as if secondary-process thought was homogeneous, a fabric that is consistently rational, rule-bound. Certainly, there is a sense in which the primary dream, the waking fantasy or reverie and the combinatory play associated with particular waking tasks do all look alike, in that they ignore the rules of physics, grammar and logic. But there are grounds for believing (i) that they are in fact quite separate components that play complementary roles within a single system; and (ii) that the relation of such components to imaginative action may differ not only from individual to individual but from task to task. The completion of a novel, the invention of a new computer program, the initiation of a new love affair, the resolution of a political crisis: each may draw on the imaginative resources of the person in question, but do so in ways that are dissimilar.

An example helps. Take the little girl already mentioned, the one with the foot fetish, and consider her for a moment, simple-mindedly, as a system rather than as a person or a patient. Three realms of imaginative activity can at once be assumed: her actions in relation to feet, what she fantasises about feet in her waking hours, and her dreams. It may well be that her fetishistic behaviour and waking fantasies gave her adequate expression. If so, her dreams could well have borne no relation to feet or fetishes. But what happens when her fetish is cured? If it disappears, and if her erotic fantasies about feet are extinguished with it, her dreams could well change. They might not deal with feet as such, but nonetheless express a concern with their erotic significance in an appropriately fragmented or metaphorical form.

Not only do such transfers of emotionally charged meaning occur; there are grounds for believing that several quite different resolutions of the same psychic instability can be reached. One resolution in the present instance is the foot fetish. Another is the state of mind and body that results when a conventional psychotherapeutic cure has taken place. Yet another is the resolution one thinks of lightly as 'creative' – conducted in terms of art, say, or personal intimacy.

What we face is not a choice between stability and instability, nor even one between healthy solutions and pathological ones. Rather, it is one among a range of configurations – each a pattern of imaginatively conceived behaviour, waking fantasy and dream, and each of which proves, after the event, to carry with it its own tariff of benefits and costs.[3]

The claim is that the psychic apparatus as a whole can take on a variety of configurations, in each of which action, fantasy and dream lock together in different but functionally equivalent ways. Nor is that all. There is evidence that the number of units, elements, components or sub-systems in play at any one time can vary. Especially when under fierce external pressure, we seem able to dissociate; and each time we dissociate, we bring a new unit or sub-system into being. A number of studies, again from the field of sexuality, show the extent of this sub-division.

We already know, on the strength of case studies like that of the little girl with a foot fetish, that the movement from one configuration to another can have consequences in the field of gender: she turned, in the course of psychotherapy from a radiant little 'boy' to a dull little girl. The whole apparatus of differentiation set out in Chapter 9, in which the various facets of maleness and femaleness are separated one from the other, can be implicated in the kinds of transformation which this little girl endured. Residual pathways – hitherto buried patterns of gender identity, object choice and presentation of self – may open of their own accord under the pressure of the psyche's internal contradictions, as they seem to have done in John Ruskin. They may also open up as part of the individual's response to some externally imposed threat or strain. In either case, they play a part in the psyche's perhaps unavailing search for equilibrium.

We also know from Robert Stoller's remarkable studies how

comprehensively sexual fantasy can become detached from sexual action. The body can be doing one thing, urgently, while its owner rehearses in the mind's eye scenes of extraordinary elaboration that are apparently quite unrelated.[4] Sexual fantasies can themselves sub-divide; those entertained as exciting in the normal course of waking life may be quite unrelated to those that arrive of their own accord as a concomitant of sexual intercourse. Sexual dreams, in turn, can be different again, both in style and personnel, either from waking sexual fantasies or from the various forms of sexual activity that the individual in question in fact undertakes.

The erotic, evidently, is an area of the human imagination subject to a surprising variety of internal divisions; and what holds for the erotic holds for the psychic apparatus as a whole. Its powers of dissociation, although subject to aberration and perhaps even to random proliferation, are in principle functional: they help the apparatus as a whole to stay, for the time being, within bounds. So eager have psychologists been in the past to condemn dissociation as unwholesome that they have failed to notice the extraordinary range of its application. It bears on the psychic apparatus itself – on the relation between dreams, waking fantasies and imaginatively conceived actions; on our personalities, and the needs, fears and identifications of which these are made up; and also on our memories. Two impulses, to dissociate and to integrate, are counterposed. Remove the tension between them and psychic energy evaporates: we have on our hands nothing more interesting than a semantic machine driven by its physiologically constituted appetites, which slips into neutral whenever these appetites are for the time being satisfied.

The suggestion that neurotic symptoms, dreams, waking fantasies and imaginatively inspired actions are dynamically related elements within the same system is, of course, a much older claim in more judicious guise: namely, that art to madness is near allied, not because artists are mad, nor because the mad are artists, but because certain sorts of people become artists (or visionary politicians, or creative scientists or impassioned lovers) as an alternative to becoming unhinged. The corollary of this argument is that if such people feel driven to act imaginatively and cannot, and if they are prevented by the wiles of the psychotherapists from becoming neurotic, remarkable things will happen either to their waking fantasies or to their dreams.

The third prong of a more circumspect reply to the dream's enemies should by now be more clearly visible. The psyche must somehow accommodate the tensions that arise when free imaginative self-expression is impossible; when, in a multifarious and often hostile world, someone cannot will a thing and then do it. Within such an accommodation, action can become dissociated from waking fantasy or reverie, one kind of waking fantasy can become dissociated from another kind, and all these can be segregated from the dream – which, in its turn, sub-divides into the thought-like and the dream-like, the secondary and the primary. The dream, it would seem to follow, is a component in a more general pattern of accommodation. At worst, it can assimilate thoughts that cannot be acted upon or acknowledged – the impulse to murder, say, or rape. More positively, it can be geared to imaginative action. Occasionally, this gearing will be direct, as in Kekulé's case. More normally, it will be indirect, as one component among several, its part on these occasions being no less valuable for being hidden.

Finally, what answer does the sceptic receive? What *would* be lost if, as a species, we had access to our waking fantasies and reveries, but could remember none of our primary dreams? The glib answer was that science and technology would have taken shape more or less as we now see them, but that artistically and personally we would have been impoverished. The more circumspect but at the same time more radical answer says, on the contrary, that waking reveries and fantasies, though sometimes odd, are rarely adequate to the psychic system's needs. Hardly ever are they sufficiently strange. Without our dreams and our limited – and, as it happens, nicely varied – access to them, we would have been too readily moulded by circumstance, too rigidly predictable, and too easily disturbed by life's necessary frustrations ever to have entertained the rigours of science or technology. Without recallable dreams, we would have been stumped for art, and stumped for science and technology too.

The fact, if it proves to be one, that the dream is an important element in our powers of adaptation does not in the least guarantee that, in fifty years time, its value will still be acknowledged, nor even that it will survive in a form that we would now recognise.

Our world is changing, and our dreams may change with it. There is a sad story told by Jung about a conversation he had in the heart of Africa with an old medicine man – a tearful old gentleman, Jung found him, in spite of a splendid cloak made from the skins of blue monkeys, 'the living embodiment of the spreading disintegration of an undermined, outmoded, unrestorable world'.[5] In the old days, the medicine men had dreams and told their people whether there was going to be war or sickness, whether the rains would come and where the herds should be driven. But since the whites had arrived in Africa, he said, no one had dreams any more. They were no longer needed because the District Commissioner knew everything.

Like the medicine man's, our present style of life and thought could quite rapidly prove outmoded, unrestorable; and in any such transformation, the dream is at risk. After two thousand years of relative stability, our attitude to the dream has recently undergone repeated upheaval. First, the notion of the dream as portent was challenged; then Freud's treatment of it as a 'royal road'. For a while a strictly behaviouristic attitude seemed entrenched, but that has now been abandoned in favour of less arbitrary 'bottom-up' theories. An uneasy truce now exists between these and more interpretative (or 'hermeneutic') views of the dream – the antagonism that this book has sought to resolve. There are grounds for suspecting that more changes of attitude are on the way, and grounds for suspecting, too, that if a new orthodoxy crystallises, it could prove less than benign.

The most obvious possibility is that, in a more sophisticated form, behaviourism will return. Both in psychology and within our culture more widely, the 'physical' could drive out the 'mental'. Progressively, the life of the mind could come to be discussed in terms of metaphors and models more appropriate to machines. Many psychologists would welcome behaviourism back, equating it with Progress, and seeing it as more socially 'hygienic' than the frames of mind it replaces. Rather than settling to the serious work of psychology, tracing the reciprocal connections between events in the mind and events in the head, and enduring the tensions implicit in such inquiry, discussion of the brain and its computer-like properties would become orthodox and all thought of the dream as interpretable would be banished to the disreputable margins of intellectual debate.

Other threats are less obvious. Some of them, it might be argued, despite its professed intentions, are ones that this book embodies. The dream could come to be seen pragmatically; as relevant or real only inasmuch as it makes itself useful by contributing to the efficiency of waking thought. Dreams, on this argument, are worth studying only if they help scientists to solve their problems or therapists to effect their cures. In earlier chapters, a conscious effort has been made to treat sleeping and waking thought as warp and weft: the threads from which an interpretative fabric is woven. All the same, it is easy to see how a more flat-footed view of the dream could become the dominant one.

Closely adjacent, there is a danger to the dream in the very effort of analysis itself. The dream is of its essence feral, and the attempt to impose *any* matrix of schemes and procedures could constitute a form of domestication. This is especially so if the analysis in question skirts around the question of the unconscious. Jacques Lacan, if he were still alive and chanced to read it, would certainly dismiss the present text as part of a cowardly Anglo-Saxon plot to diminish the terror and strangeness of the unconscious processes that shape our dreams; a conspiracy to drain the unconscious of its life-giving powers of subversion and surprise. The psychologist's task, from this point of vantage, is not to be reasonable about Unreason. It is to manufacture texts in which the barriers between conscious and unconscious are slyly breached: mirrors that are windows and windows that mirror – reflective surfaces, like those of surreal works of art, into which we can each peer. Such criticism is often glib and self-congratulatory. It would still be foolish to deny the harm that sweet reason can do: a psychic blight spread across our awareness of our own thought.

If a surfeit of common sense and a surfeit of theorising both threaten the dream's vitality, the most potent of the dangers it faces may yet come from another source altogether: all around us, in the rapidly evolving world of machines.

In such a context, it is easy to sound like a Luddite. That is not my intention. The relation of man to his machines is subtle. Some machines are merely useful; but there are others – and the camera, television set and computer are all prime examples – that in addition to their utility alter our imaginative range, opening certain avenues unexpectedly and, equally unexpectedly, closing others. Such changes create complex equations of cost and benefit, and their more important sequelae are typically unforeseen.

Of the machines that endanger the dream, the most apparent is the television set. This instrument, with its jumpy conjunctions of image with image, narrative snippet with narrative snippet, has already made part of our everyday experience a state of mind that is in important respects dream-like. At first glance, this revolution is one that should strengthen the grip of the primary processes upon us, and slacken those of common sense and the narrative mode. It is someone else's 'dreams', though, to which the television inures us; its thrills are manageable and its messages predigested. When bored or threatened, we can switch them off. In comparison, real dreams – elusive and by no means anodyne – make demands both on our powers of introspective concentration and on our ability to tolerate ambiguity that the television set could soon have rendered obsolete.

It might be said that the human race will need to retain these powers, if only to ensure that those who work in television can go on manufacturing 'dreams' for the rest of us to watch. But even this argument has an unpleasant corollary: that the new technologies of communication and representation could rapidly prove divisive, separating the technically competent from their audience – a proletariat of the spirit whose role is passively to watch and enjoy.

Equally discomforting prospects are offered by another machine, as yet in its infancy, but in the long run more threatening to the dream perhaps even than the television set: namely, the computer. Within the next two or three generations of computers, the power to initiate may already have begun to pass from clever people to clever machines. In such a world, it is machines, not people, who become the focus of fascination and allure. Our minds, like bureaucracies, could retain the ability to proliferate within established rules, but lose the ability to impose new orders on the world in the light of imaginatively perceived needs. Within such a regime, our position would be closely akin to Jung's medicine man. Just as he found it pointless to consult his own intuitive processes of thought, so too would we.

Whatever form it takes, evolutionary change is characteristically blind, it seems. As Gould points out, the data of evolution force us to uncouple the notion of change from that of an enlightening advance:

'Adaptation, be it biological or cultural, represents a better fit to specific, local environments, not an inevitable stage in a ladder of progress. . . . Wheels, like wings, fins, and brains, are exquisite devices for certain purposes, not signs of intrinsic superiority.'[6]

The fact that the brain has evolved the ability to dream, and the likelihood that the dream is integral to our powers of adaptation, by no means guarantees its survival. With the advent of the new machines, our ability to consult our own imaginative processes could atrophy. We could become creatures for whom the dream had the same semantic status as the hiccough.

The dream is a potential casualty of technological advance, and the evidence of the last half-century is that a lethal encroachment may already have begun. As with any wilderness, the dream's benefits are rarely tangible; and at a given moment, it is impossible for the coloniser – like the property developer, high on the adventure of cement – to know what it is that he might expunge. If processes of thought can be considered as habitats, the dream is among the endangered ones. Accordingly, there is an argument in favour of its protection; even for a consciously cultivated spirit of conservation. The dream, this suggests, should be guarded at least as fervently as we now guard Georgian architecture or the highland gorilla. A commitment to protect and celebrate is, in practice, always a matter of faith, however. It is appropriate, therefore, that what is in effect a plea on the dream's behalf should be attached to the main body of this text in the form of a coda, and that it should be marked off in terms of its style. The remaining chapter is offered obliquely. Those who already know what value they put on the dream, or who are irritated by metaphors and allegories, are at liberty to move straight on to the references and index at the end.

Notes

(1) I am grateful, at this point in the argument, to Edward de Bono for a passing nudge in the right direction.

(2) The part played by surrealism in the relation to one another of dreams, psychoanalysis and the arts of poetry, painting, photography and film-making is one of this text's casualties: it deserves more space than in the end it receives.

(3) 'Waking fantasy' is here used as shorthand for all those states of mind that we entertain while awake and that are set at a distance from common sense. The question of whether they are conscious, partially conscious or unconscious is seen, in the present context, as an irrelevance.

(4) Stoller (1979).

(5) Jung (1983), p. 294.

(6) Gould (1983), p. 159. The imaginative significance of new machines is a theme broached in Hudson (1983), with special reference to the camera.

CHAPTER THIRTEEN

An Ethnographic Coda

In Darwin's time, Patagonia still occupied the place it had held for centuries in the minds of educated Europeans: a land of fable, full of giants and monsters. Its fauna included the succurath, a creature with the head of a lion and a tail armed with sharp bristles that served as a shelter for its young; and the yaquaru or water-tiger, that lived in whirlpools and was probably a caiman. These animals merged in the minds of naturalists like Cuvier with the mylodon, a real but extinct species whose bones Charles Darwin collected on a Patagonian beach, and packed off to the Royal College of Surgeons.

Visiting them in the 1830s aboard the *Beagle*, Darwin found the wildernesses of Patagonia a source of lasting fascination. But even then, the character of the region was beginning to change. The Indians were being killed off, and those that survived were driven into the countryside's margins. The ranchers were extending their domain; and Patagonia was becoming a refuge, too, for those fleeing from war and religious persecution the world over. It was also a dumping ground for misfits, maniacs and criminals. Swedes, Boers, Lithuanians, Germans, North Americans, Spaniards arrived there singly or in small bands; there also arrived boatloads of Scots and Welsh. In 1865, 153 Welsh landed from the brig *Mimosa*, poor people in search of a New Wales, fugitives from the coal-mining valleys, from an independence movement that had aborted, and from the Westminster government's ban on the teaching of Welsh in schools. Their leaders had combed the earth 'for a stretch of open country uncontaminated by Englishmen'.[1] As a result, the last refuge of the Welsh language may prove to lie, not in Wales, but in the Welsh villages of what is now southern Argentina. As with those Welsh expatriates, so with the contents of our sleeping heads: it does not follow from our ignorance of them that they are not there.

With the spread of ranching, the Indians took to cattle rustling, and men with a sense of destiny like Argentina's General Rosas did their best to exterminate them. Darwin, initially charmed by Rosas, was horrified: those who resisted were shot, as was any male who gave himself up and seemed unlikely to be useful as an informant. The better-looking girls were set aside for the soldiery, and the older women and the uglier girls were murdered. The children were sold off as slaves.[2] By the time the Christian missionaries had established a foothold, this policy was in a significant respect modified: the remaining Indians were rounded up, taught about Christ's love in the mission house, and allowed to die there of alien germs.

The work of exterminating the Indians still outside the mission, and still rustling cattle, was carried on at the turn of the century by ranch managers like Alexander MacLennan, a Scot who had served as a sergeant with Kitchener at Omdurman and who came to be known by the Indians as the 'Red Pig'. A man loved by his farmhands and dogs, he wearied of the attrition achieved in the mission house, and settled on a more forthright solution: he shot the Indians as game.[3]

All this was recent enough to permit the traveller Bruce Chatwin, attending the Baptist church one Sunday in Punta Arenas in the 1970s, to meet there an old Highland shepherd called Black Bob MacDonald who had once worked for MacLennan: 'Grand man!' he is reported to have said. Also living peacefully in Punta Arenas at that time was a man who 'dreams pine forests, hums Lieder' and drives each morning to 'a factory that smells of the sea. All about him are scarlet crabs, crawling, then steaming,' soon to be packed into cans. Called Herman Rauff, an orderly man, he was credited with the invention and administration of the Mobile Gas Oven.[4]

The naivety of the earlier colonisers, as seen after an interval of only a century or so, is as breath-taking as was their brutality. On the *Beagle* with Darwin were three Indians from Tierra del Fuego whom the ship's captain, Robert Fitzroy, had kidnapped in the course of an earlier voyage: Jemmy Button, York Minster and a girl, Fuegia Basket. Fitzroy's assumption was that, having dressed Jemmy in fashionable English clothes, shown him to the Royal Family, and sent him to a boarding school in Walthamstow to learn the Christian virtues, he could then release him again among his own people, and that Christianity would spread like wildfire up through Patagonia from its tip.

No such thing happened, needless to say. The London Missionary Society had equipped Jemmy, York and Fuegia for their return with, among other items, chamber pots, tea trays and crockery, wine glasses and soup tureens, and white linen. When the *Beagle* returned a year later, York and Fuegia were nowhere to be seen. Jemmy had married, but was now no longer the Jemmy that Darwin and Fitzroy knew: as Darwin said, 'Instead of the clean, well-dressed stout lad we left him, we found him a naked thin squalid savage.' Fitzroy pleaded with Jemmy to stay on board the *Beagle* and leave squalor and paganism behind, but he wisely refused. Twenty-five years later, and in his own way, he took his revenge. He staged a massacre of eight white missionaries in the Anglican church that the Patagonian Missionary Society had then set up in his homeland. After that, he lived on a few more years into the 1870s, and witnessed the first of the epidemics that were to wipe his people out.[5]

The elimination of an indigenous population, carried out by men acting in good faith, in the name of progress, is only the setting for this story's central concern, which is with language – or, more strictly, with the consciousness that language contains.

Thomas Bridges was an English orphan. Born in 1863, he was adopted by the Rev. George Despard, a Nottinghamshire clergyman who was secretary to the Patagonian Mission Society, and who took Bridges out, while still a boy, to the Falkland Islands. From there, Bridges crossed the sea to Tierra del Fuego, where he took over from the men that Jemmy Button and his band had murdered. As a young man, he decided to learn the language of the local Indians, not as an end in itself, but as a means to an end: he wanted to tell them, 'to my satisfaction and their conviction of the love of Jesus'.[6]

Darwin had been told by Jemmy that the Fuego Indians were cannibals, although Bridges was later to deny this. Certainly, he formed an unfavourable impression of both them and their language: 'the most abject and miserable creatures', whom he could scarcely bring himself to believe were 'fellow creatures and inhabitants of the same world', using a language that 'scarcely deserves to be called articulate'. Fitzroy, likewise, had seen little to praise in them: one of the three local tribes he describes as 'satires upon mankind . . . the miserable lords of this miserable land'. They had small distorted bodies, and the women combed their hair with the jaws of porpoises: 'she-Fuegians – by courtesy called women'. In contrast the tribe whom Darwin first met were tall, with long, matted hair and dark cadaverous faces, painted in stripes of red and black, with white circles around the eyes. The colour of their skin was copper, they covered themselves with grease, and apart from a short mantle of fur over their shoulders, were naked.[7]

The language of the Fuego Indians proved more elaborate than it seemed at first sight, however, and out of Bridges' zeal grew a dictionary. Sitting with an Indian called George Okkoko, he listed, in the end, some 32,000 words, without exhausting Okkoko's powers of expression. Bridges' dictionary is now the only indication left of what it was that the missionaries, the Red Pig and the epidemics expunged.[8]

Despite his patience, Bridges in the end despaired of finding in the Indians' language, a 'labyrinth of the particular', any words with which to convey the more abstract and intangible notions of the Gospel. In their own way, though, the riches of the language were vast. In it, ideas, rather than being referred to directly and given verbal labels, emerge as synonyms for more literal verbs and nouns.

Some of these synonyms still speak to us directly. The Indians conveyed the notion of monotony, for instance, as 'an absence of male friends'; depression by using the word that describes the vulnerable phase in a crab's seasonal cycle, when it has shed its old shell and waits for a new one to grow and harden; adultery by reference to the hobby, the small falcon that darts swiftly to and fro, swooping suddenly on its next victim.

There are in addition synonyms that lure the outsider into a way of life that is strange, but, within its own terms, intelligible:

sleet = fish scales
fuel = something burned = cancer
mussels out of season = shrivelled skin = old age

Others seem at first sight inscrutable, but then, with an imaginative stride, make sense. For instance:

a bog = mortal wound

The bogs of Tierra del Fuego, as Chatwin points out, are mattresses of moss, oozing water; their colour a dull yellow with reddish smears, the colour of an open and putrefying wound. The bogs, too, are laid out flat across valley floors, like a fatally wounded man. Many synonyms remain opaque, however. One can only guess at the connections, substantial or more fleeting, that brought about, for example, the verbal equation:

fur seal = relatives of a murdered man

The Indians' language, moreover, is one in which primacy belongs not to the nouns, but to verbs. Resembling 'fidgety birds of passage, who feel happy and inwardly calm only when they are on the move', the Indians needed to differentiate not so much their objects as their activities. There is a specific word that means 'moor your canoe to a streamer of kelp'; and a specific word, too, for sleeping in a canoe, as opposed to sleeping in a hut, on a beach, or with your wife. Verbs beget nouns: the word for skeleton comes from 'to gnaw thoroughly'. And verbs gather activities into clans:

To be loose or easily moved, as a broken bone or the blade of a knife = to wander about or roam, as a homeless or lost child = to be attached yet loose, as an eye or bone in its socket = to swing, move or travel = to exist or be

Bridges coined his name for the tribe, Yaghan, after a place name, Yagha. The Indians called themselves *Yámana*. Used as a verb, *yámana* means 'to live, breathe, be happy, recover from sickness or be sane'. As a noun it designates people as opposed to animals. As a suffix it indicates friendliness: a hand offered in friendship, for example, as opposed to a claw.

In search of Yaghan survivors, Chatwin was directed to some shanties at the far end of a Chilean naval base on Navarino Island. Grandpa Felipe, he was told, was the only 'pure-blood' left. He had been born in the Anglican Mission and was probably related to Jemmy Button. He had always been ill, and he watched the rest die around him: his friends, his wife, all his children with the

175

exception of a daughter. He had the face of a Mongol, and black unmoving eyes; and earned a little money, now and again, making canoes for the occasional tourist. He also whittled miniature harpoons.

What are the morals of all this for the study of dreams? One is tempted to list them: little Roman one, little Roman two, little Roman three. . . . But, for once, they should perhaps be left to speak for themselves.

Notes

(1) This chapter draws heavily on Bruce Chatwin's brilliantly evocative book, *In Patagonia* (1979).
(2) Moorehead (1971), p. 97.
(3) Chatwin (1979), p. 111.
(4) Ibid., p. 185.
(5) Ibid., p. 121, Moorehead (1971), p. 83.
(6) Chatwin (1979), p. 128. Fitzroy was sufficiently interested in the Fuegians' language to include a vocabulary of their various dialects in an appendix to his narrative of the *Beagle*'s voyage.
(7) Moorehead (1971), pp. 72–9.
(8) Chatwin (1979), pp. 128–31, Hestermann and Gusinde (1933). The dictionary's subsequent history was suitably chequered. It was filched by Frederick Cook, an American doctor who travelled with the Belgian Antarctic Expedition in 1898, the year of Bridges' death. Cook subsequently tried to pass if off as his own work. He also claimed to have beaten Peary to the North Pole. He died as recently as 1940, having served a prison sentence for selling forged oil shares. The manuscript, though published in a limited edition in Austria in 1933, was lost in Germany during the Second World War, only to be recovered by Sir Leonard Woolley, the excavator of Ur, and presented to the British Museum.

References

Aleksander, I., *Reinventing Man* (London: Kogan Page, 1983).

Austin, M., 'Dream recall and the bias of intellectual ability', *Nature*, 231 (1971), p. 59.

Barthes, R., *A Lover's Discourse* (London: Cape, 1979).

Bartlett, F. C., *Remembering* (Cambridge: Cambridge University Press, 1932).

Bowie, M., 'Jacques Lacan', in *Structuralism and Since*, ed. J. Sturrock (Oxford: Oxford University Press, 1979).

Broadbent, J., 'Marvell, symbol, structure and satire', in *From Donne to Marvell*, ed. B. Ford (Harmondsworth: Penguin, 1982).

Brome, V., *Jung* (London: Macmillan, 1978).

Brook, S., *The Oxford Book of Dreams* (Oxford: Oxford University Press, 1983).

Chatwin, B., *In Patagonia* (London: Picador, 1979).

Cohen, D. B., *Sleep and Dreaming* (Oxford: Pergamon, 1979).

Cormack, M. and Sheldrake, P. F., *Cognitive Bias and Patterns in Dream Recall*, Occasional Paper 18 (Edinburgh: Centre for Research in the Educational Sciences, 1974).

Craik, K., *The Nature of Explanation* (Cambridge: Cambridge University Press, 1943).

Crick, F. H. C. and Mitchison, G., 'The function of dream sleep', *Nature*, 304 (1983), p. 111.

Darwin, C., *The Descent of Man*, 1st edition (London: Murray, 1871).

Darwin, C., *The Descent of Man*, 2nd edition (London: Murray, 1887).

Dodds, E. R., *The Greeks and the Irrational* (Berkeley: University of California Press, 1951).

Doolittle, W. F. and Sapienza, C., 'Selfish genes, the phenotype paradigm and genome evolution', *Nature*, 284 (1980), p. 601.

Eliot, T. S., *Selected Prose* (Harmondsworth: Penguin, 1953).

Evans, C., *Landscapes of the Night*, ed. P. Evans (London: Gollancz, 1983).

Farrell, J. G., *The Siege of Krishnapur* (Harmondsworth: Penguin, 1975).

Farrell, J. G., *The Singapore Grip* (Harmondsworth: Penguin, 1978).

Foulkes, D., *A Grammar of Dreams* (London: Harvester, 1978).

Foulkes, D. and Pope, R., 'PVE and SCE in stage REM', *Perceptual and Motor Skills*, 37 (1973), p. 107.

177

Gass, W., *On Being Blue* (Boston: Godine, 1976).

Getzels, J. W. and Jackson, P. W., *Creativity and Intelligence* (New York: Wiley, 1962).

Gould, S. J., *Hen's Teeth and Horse's Toes* (New York: Norton, 1983).

Gould, S. J. and Lewontin, R. C., 'The spandrels of San Marco and the Panglossian paradigm', *Proceedings of the Royal Society, London*, B.205 (1979), p. 581.

Greene, G., *Ways of Escape* (Harmondsworth: Penguin, 1981).

Gregory, R. L., *Eye and Brain* (London: Weidenfeld, 1966).

Habermas, J., *Knowledge and Human Interests* (London: Heinemann, 1972).

Hadamard, J., *The Psychology of Invention in the Mathematical Field* (Princeton: Princeton University Press, 1945).

Hestermann, F. and Gusinde, M., *Yámana – English Dictionary* (Mödling, 1933).

Hobson, J. A., 'Film and the physiology of dreaming sleep', *Dreamworks*, 1 (1980), p. 9.

Holmes, M. A. M., *REM Sleep Patterning and Dream Recall in Convergers and Divergers*, Occasional Paper 16 (Edinburgh: Centre for Research in the Educational Sciences, 1973).

Holmes, M. A. M., 'REM sleep patterning and dream recall in convergers and divergers', PhD thesis, Edinburgh University (1976).

Hopfield, J. J., Feinstein, D. I. and Palmer, R. G., ' "Unlearning" has a stabilizing effect in collective memories', *Nature*, 304 (1983), p. 158.

Hopkins, J., 'The probable role of trauma in a case of foot and shoe fetishism', *International Review of Psychoanalysis*, 11 (1984), p. 79.

Hudson, L., *Contrary Imaginations* (London: Methuen, 1966).

Hudson, L., 'The stereotypical scientist', *Nature* 213 (1967), p. 228.

Hudson, L., *Frames of Mind* (London: Methuen, 1968).

Hudson, L., *The Cult of the Fact* (London: Cape, 1972).

Hudson, L., 'Fertility in the arts and sciences', *Science Studies*, 3 (1973), p. 305.

Hudson, L., *Human Beings* (London: Cape, 1975).

Hudson, L., *Bodies of Knowledge* (London: Weidenfeld, 1982).

Hudson, L., *The Great Misceganation* (London: Society of Industrial Artists and Designers, 1983).

Hudson, L., 'Psychology', in *Social Sciences Encyclopaedia*, ed. A. Kuper and J. Kuper (London: Routledge & Kegan Paul, in press).

Hudson, L. and Jacot, B., 'Marriage and fertility in academic life', *Nature* 229 (1971), p. 283.

Hudson, L., and Jacot, B., 'The outsider in science', in *Personality, Cognition and Values*, ed. C. Bagley and G. K. Verma (London: Macmillan, 1985).

Hudson, L., Jacot, B. and Sheldrake, P. F., *Lieben und Arbeiten: Patterns of*

Work and Patterns of Marriage, Occasional Paper 12 (Edinburgh: Centre for Research in the Educational Sciences, 1973).

Hudson, L., Johnston J. and Jacot, B., *Perception and Communication in Academic Life*, Occasional Paper 8 (Edinburgh: Centre for Research in the Educational Sciences, 1972).

Jaynes, J., *The Origin of Consciousness in the Breakdown of the Bicameral Mind* (Boston: Houghton Mifflin, 1976).

Jones, E., *The Life and Work of Sigmund Freud* (London: Hogarth, 1961).

Jung, C. G., *Man and his Symbols* (London: Aldus, 1964).

Jung, C. G., *Memories, Dreams, Reflections* (London: Fontana, 1983).

Kinder, M., 'The adaptation of cinematic dreams', *Dreamworks*, 1 (1980), p. 54.

Koestler, A., *The Sleepwalkers* (London: Hutchinson, 1959).

Kuhn, T. S., 'The essential tension: tradition and innovation in scientific research', in *Scientific Creativity*, ed. C. W. Taylor and F. Barron (New York: Wiley, 1963).

Kuper, A., 'The structure of dream sequences', in *Culture, Medicine and Psychiatry*, 7 (1983), p. 153.

Kuper, A. and Stone, A., 'The dream of Irma's injection: a structural account', *American Journal of Psychiatry*, 139 (1982), p. 1225.

Lakoff, G. and Johnson, M., *Metaphors We Live By* (Chicago: Chicago University Press, 1980).

Lashley, K. S., 'Cerebral organisation and behaviour', in *The Brain and Human Behaviour*, ed. H. C. Solomon, S. Cobb and W. Penfield (Baltimore, Md: Proceedings of the Association for Research in Nervous and Mental Disease, vol. 36, 1958).

Latour, B. and Woolgar, S., *Laboratory Life* (Beverley Hills: Sage, 1979).

Leishman, J. B., *Sonnets to Orpheus, Rainer Maria Rilke* (London: Hogarth, 1949).

Leishman, J. B., *Rilke: Selected Poems* (Harmondsworth: Penguin, 1964).

Leslie, A., *The Rhododendron Handbook* (London: The Royal Horticultural Society, 1980).

Leupold-Löwenthal, H. and Lobner, H., *Sigmund Freud – House Catalogue* (Vienna: Löcker & Wögenstein, 1975).

McKellar, P., *Mindsplit* (London: Dent, 1979).

Maudsley, H., *The Physiology and Pathology of the Mind* (London: Macmillan, 1868).

Molinari, S. and Foulkes, D., 'Tonic and phasic events during sleep', *Perceptual and Motor Skills*, 29 (1969), p. 343.

Moorehead, A., *Darwin and the Beagle* (Harmondsworth: Penguin, 1971).

Orgel, L. E. and Crick, F. H. C., 'Selfish DNA: the ultimate parasite', *Nature*, 284 (1980), p. 604.

Oswald, I., *Sleep* (Harmondsworth: Penguin, 1980).

Painter, G. D., *Marcel Proust* (Harmondsworth: Penguin, 1983).

Powell, A., *The Military Philosophers* (London: Fontana, 1971).

Powell, A., *Temporary Kings* (London: Fontana, 1974).

Pribram, K. H. and Gill, M. M. *Freud's Project Re-Assessed* (New York: Basic Books, 1976).

Rechtschaffen, A., 'The control of sleep', in *Human Behaviour and its Control*, ed. W. A. Hunt (Cambridge, Mass.: Schenkman, 1971).

Rhys, J., *Smile Please* (Harmondsworth: Penguin, 1981).

Rieff, P., *Freud: The Mind of a Moralist* (New York: Viking, 1959).

Roazen, P., *Freud and his Followers* (New York: Knopf, 1975).

Robinson, F. N., *The Poetic Works of Chaucer* (Oxford: Oxford University Press, no date).

Rosenberg, J. D., *The Darkening Glass* (London: Routledge & Kegan Paul, 1963).

Rycroft, C., *The Innocence of Dreams* (London: Hogarth, 1979).

Saint-Denys, H. de, *Dreams and How to Guide Them*, ed. M. Schatzman (London: Duckworth, 1981).

Shepard, O., *The Lore of the Unicorn* (London: Allen & Unwin, 1930).

Stoller, R. J., *Perversion* (London: Harvester, 1976).

Stoller, R. J., *Sexual Excitement* (New York: Pantheon, 1979).

Storr, A., *Jung: Selected Writings* (London: Fontana, 1983).

Strachey, J. (trans.), *The Interpretation of Dreams, by Sigmund Freud* (London: Allen & Unwin, 1954).

Sulloway, F. J., *Freud, Biologist of Mind* (London: Burnett, 1979).

Sulloway, F. J., 'Darwin and his finches', in *Journal of the History of Biology*, 15 (1982), p. 1.

Vonnegut, K., *Palm Sunday* (London: Granada, 1982).

White, R., *The Interpretation of Dreams: The Oneirocritica of Artemidorus* (Park Ridge, NY: Noyes, 1975).

Woodcock, A. and Davis, M., *Catastrophe Theory* (Harmondsworth: Penguin, 1980).

Yates, F., *The Art of Memory* (Harmondsworth: Penguin, 1969).

Zuckerman, H., *Scientific Elite* (New York: Free Press, 1977).

Index